# READY, SET, LEAD!

# READY, SET, LEAD!

## The New Pastor's Guide to Starting Ministry

### LYNDA C. WARD

### STEVEN P. BREY

Abingdon Press
*Nashville*

**READY, SET, LEAD**
**THE NEW PASTOR'S GUIDE TO STARTING MINISTRY**

*Copyright © 2006 by Abingdon Press*

All rights reserved.

*This book is printed on acid-free paper.*

### Library of Congress Cataloging-in-Publication Data

Ward, Lynda C., 1963-
    Ready, set, lead: the new pastor's guide to starting ministry / Lynda C. Ward and Steven P. Brey.
    p. cm.
    ISBN 0-687-49610-1 (pbk. : alk. paper)
    1. Pastoral theology.    I. Brey, Steven P. (Steven Phillip) II. Title.
    BV4011.3.W37 2006
    253—dc22

                            2005019460

06 07 08 09 10 11 12 13 14 15—10 9 8 7 6 5 4 3 2 1

MANUFACTURED IN THE UNITED STATES OF AMERICA

*To* Nancy and Davis Ward for their

continuous and generous support over

the years, and to Lambs Chapel United

Methodist Church, LaPorte, Indiana,

for showing us true Christian hospitality

# CONTENTS

# BEGIN WITH DISCERNMENT

It is difficult to write a guidebook for new pastors and offer advice without sounding preachy. So we turn to a recommendation once given by a wise retiring pastor to his young successor: "Practice discernment. Notice everything."

He was right. While the excitement of beginning a new ministry should not be overlooked, caution is needed. Prayer and discernment are necessary in order to set appropriate goals. What is it that you want to accomplish? Together with members of your new church, how can you realize what it means to "put your faith into practice"?

*Ready, Set, Lead* offers the essential tools and strategies that you will need to set appropriate priorities for your first year. It is packed with practical advice, wisdom from experienced pastors, reproducible pages, and checklists. These valuable resources—both creative and pragmatic—are ones that you can use again and again while you grow as a faithful and faith-filled minister and a steward of Christ's church.

Together, then, let us embark upon a journey to discover what is most important in the context of your calling to be a pastor in the local church.

# CHAPTER ONE

# GET STARTED

David Holmes received his call to ministry in his third year of college, while volunteering at a food pantry and participating in a Bible study with some of the other volunteers. So after college David went on to study theology. Then late one May afternoon, he got the phone call; he would be the new pastor of Cedar Bend Church. After he shared the good news with his family and friends, he wondered what he should do first: Write the sermon for his first Sunday? Get ready to move into the parsonage? Visit some of his new parishioners? He didn't know where to begin.

Preparing to be the pastor at a new church is similar to preparing for a year-long journey. No one gets in a car and starts out on a long holiday without first making preparations. The same is true with ministry. Before you begin, you will need to pack some essentials and chart out a course for the days ahead.

## Identify Your Interests

A loal church pastor wears many hats. He or she equips the congregation for Christian ministry by preaching the Word and administering the sacraments, providing guidance and comfort to members, and overseeing the administrative life of the church. But no pastor can be an expert at every task, so knowing which type of ministry you are called to is important because the more you know about yourself and your particular preferences, the more enthusiasm and focus you can bring to your ministry.

To which type of ministry are you called? Since you are reading this book, you might answer, "I am called to local church ministry," but be more specific. What is your ministry specialty? What are your strengths? What are some of the obstacles that might stand in your way?

Consider and circle the two areas of ministry that interest you most:

Preaching                                  Age-specific Ministries (e.g., ministry
Liturgy                                          with children or seniors)
Teaching                                   Charitable Outreach / Missions
Administration                             Evangelical Outreach / Membership
Administration                             Other: _____
Specialty or Alternative
     Ministries

In order to identify your strengths in these areas and some of the challenges that might stand in your way, please write your two choices below, then list the gifts and talents that you bring to each ministry.

Choice #1: _____

The gifts and talents you bring to this specific area of ministry (strengths):

_____
_____
_____
_____

Personal obstacles that might stand in your way (challenges):

_____
_____
_____
_____

Choice #2: _____

The gifts and talents you bring to this specific area of ministry (strengths):

_____
_____
_____
_____

Personal obstacles that might stand in your way (challenges):

_____
_____
_____
_____

# Write Your Personal Ministry Statement

Many ministers like to begin each new ministry by writing a personal ministry statement and setting a couple of simple and achievable goals.

A personal ministry statement can be a valuable tool to give direction in your first year. Your statement can also help you evaluate your progress at the end of the year. For an example, let's look at what David Holmes wrote:

> I believe I am called to local church ministry, but I am especially passionate about missions and small group ministry. My strengths are my organizational skills, my ability to work with others as a team member, my outgoing personality, and my desire to share God's love with everyone I meet. I am not a strong leader, but I want to strengthen my leadership skills. Because I am a focused person, sometimes my passion for one aspect of ministry leads me to neglect other areas of ministry. I'll need to be sure to remind myself that balance is the key to being a faithful and effective leader of a church.

What is your personal ministry statement? Write it below:

_____

_____

_____

_____

_____

_____

# Set Some Short-term Goals

Now that you have identified your specific interests and written your ministry statement, set a couple of short-term goals for the upcoming year. Note: These are your *personal* goals, not goals for your new church to accomplish. For example, Pastor Holmes chose one goal that focused on one of his strengths and another that focused on one of his challenges:

1. Offer a month-long sermon series on the importance of charitable outreach and missions in the life of the church.
2. Do two things in the coming year to strengthen leadership skills. For example, study a book on leadership skills and attend a leadership training workshop or conference.

In the space below, write two goals that you want to accomplish in the first year of your ministry. Remember, keep them simple:

1. _____
_____
_____

2. _____
_____
_____

# Introduce Yourself to Your New Church

One of the best ways to introduce yourself to your new church is to write a letter of introduction. This is a brief, no more than two pages, double-spaced, typed letter that allows each member of your parish to get to know you better. Typically a letter of introduction includes a brief biographical history (including something about your call to ministry), educational history, and a greeting that lets the members know that you look forward to meeting them and are excited about serving as their new pastor. If you are married and have children, include something about your spouse's profession or interests and your children's ages and hobbies. The letter should be positive in tone and general in the information it offers.

In terms of mailing your letter, the names and addresses of your church's members can be found in the current membership directory—ask a church leader to get you a copy. If the membership is small enough, hand addressing each letter adds a personal touch, but if this is not feasible, find out if the church has a set of preprinted address labels for you to use. You can make the letter more personable by enclosing a recent photo of yourself or a small token, such as a bookmark with a Bible verse printed on it. Try to mail your letter of introduction *two weeks* before your first Sunday. Remember, some members will be nervous about meeting you. A letter of introduction will help put these members at ease.

# Introduce Yourself to the Local Community

A great way to introduce yourself to the community and to invite members of the community to attend your new church is to send a press release to local newspapers. A press release is more formal than a letter of introduction and is much shorter, usually no more than 300 words. It should be typed, single-spaced, on plain white business paper. Here is Pastor David Holmes's press release:

Press Release: For Immediate Release
(put current date here)
Cedar Bend Church Welcomes New Pastor
David T. Holmes is the new pastor of Cedar Bend Church. David is twenty-seven years old and comes to Cedar Bend from Columbus, Ohio, where he recently completed his studies in ministry. Born in Lexington, Kentucky, Pastor Holmes attended the University of Kentucky where he majored in history and was active in a community food pantry. While volunteering at this food pantry, Holmes received his call to ministry.

Upon hearing that he would be the new pastor at Cedar Bend Church, Holmes said, "I'm so excited, and I'm looking forward to moving to Cedar Bend and meeting the members of Cedar Bend Church, as well as the members of the Cedar Bend Community. I'd like to invite everyone to join me for worship my first Sunday, July 16, at 9:30 A.M."

In addition to his interests in Christian mission and outreach, Holmes enjoys playing softball, and he fancies himself quite the chef. His specialties include backyard barbecues and making a "mean chili." He is married to Becky Holmes, a paralegal who will be working at the law offices of McGraffe and Centnor in Hillington.

Press releases can also be sent to specialty and community newspapers, magazines, and radio stations, especially Christian radio stations. Be sure to include a current phone number and e-mail address for further contact, should they have questions or want to do a formal interview. If you have a photo of yourself, include it or mention that a photo is available. Press releases should be mailed *one month* in advance of your first Sunday.

# Meet with Key Leaders of the Church

A casual meeting over breakfast or for coffee with two or three of your church's key leaders or important staff members will help you become familiar with your church's history and its current needs. And by listening carefully and asking some pertinent questions, you can pick up some ideas for your first sermon: small bits of church trivia that will make your first sermon more personal and particular. As you meet with leaders, remember to keep the focus on them. This is not the time to share your plans or vision—instead, your role at this meeting is to listen.

Here are some questions you might want to ask:

1. *Strengths:* What does the church do well? Where and in what ways do they see God present and at work in the parish? What aspect of worship is especially meaningful to them? What are the annual events in the life of the parish to which people look forward?
2. *Challenges:* What particular obstacles do they face? What is their greatest challenge? If they were to give one piece of advice to their new minister, what would it be?
3. *Opportunities:* In what areas are they, as a church, still learning and growing? What are a few things they would like to accomplish in the coming year? What are some of the ways that you can be helpful to them?

In addition, here are some more specific, business-related questions to ask about your move and to help you get organized:

1. Can someone give you a list of members who are homebound, seriously ill, recently bereaved, a list of new members, and a list of any visitors from the past few months?
2. Can someone get you copies of old bulletins, newsletters, and if there is a written church history, a copy of that history?
3. What is the schedule for cleaning and repairing the parsonage? Since most parsonage repairs are made between pastoral moves, ask about coordinating your move with their cleaning and repair schedule. (This might mean delaying your move or staying in a hotel while they clean the carpets or paint the walls.)
4. Is there a deadline for turning in information for the church's bulletin and newsletter? (You will want to get your first sermon title and any other information in on time.)
5. Is there anything else you've forgotten to ask them? Is there anything important that they feel you should know?

It is also essential to meet with the people involved with the worship service, especially the music ministry, as soon as possible, to discuss how the service will be coordinated, who will be participating, and who will select the hymns: the pastor? the pianist? the choir director? Or will these duties be shared?

# Put Your Best Foot Forward

First impressions are important. As you meet with your church's leaders and members, you will begin to get to know them, and they will begin to get to know you. The key to making a good impression is to be honest and willing to disclose appropriate information about yourself while maintaining a sense of professionalism. Prior to meeting any of the members at your new church, decide what information you want to share and what you want to hold back until you have had more time to build personal relationships. Think of this as similar to attending a party at a new friend's house, and try to strike a balance between revealing too little and too much. Remember, you only get to make a first impression once, so put your best foot forward.

# Prepare the Message for Your First Sunday

Your first sermon introduces you to your new congregation, so prepare it with care. Most pastors find it easier to prepare their first message prior to the chaos of moving and the busyness of their first week of ministry.

Preaching to a congregation whom you do not know and who does not know you might seem a bit daunting, but it doesn't have to be. Your new congregation will be eager to learn something about you, your call to ministry, and what you love about being a minister. They will also want to hear that you are pleased to be serving their church and that you are looking forward to working with them, no matter who they are or where they are in their spiritual journey.

As you prepare your introductory sermon, here are some suggested dos and don'ts:

- *Do* keep the tone positive and upbeat, but *don't* try to be funny or overly serious. This is not the time to make heavy political statements. (You might be against the death penalty, but now is not the time to share it.)
- *Do* take a deep breath and deliver the message in a relaxed manner, but *don't* try to cram all your thoughts into one sermon. Keep it around fifteen minutes.
- *Do* share something of your call to ministry and your faith, but *don't* get too personal in disclosing information about yourself.
- *Do* let them know that you are glad to be with them, but *don't* promise things that you can't deliver.
- *Do* demonstrate that you know something about them and their church, but *don't* share your specific plans or vision for the church. There'll be time for that later.

In terms of content for your first sermon, think back to your meeting with the church's leaders. Was there something you learned that you could use in your first sermon to make your message more personal and particular to this congregation? For an example, let's turn again to Pastor Holmes:

> After his casual breakfast meeting with a few of the leaders from Cedar Bend Church, David looked over his notes and thought about his first sermon. He had already planned briefly to share something about himself and his call to ministry, and he also had considered using Hebrews 13:2 ("Do not neglect to show hospitality to strangers, for by doing that some have entertained angels without knowing it") to show how working at the food pantry had been a turning point in his life. And since the church was welcoming him as their new pastor, he felt hospitality was a timely topic.
>
> But now he needed something to make his first message particular to Cedar Bend Church. He flipped through his notes, but it wasn't something in his notes that caught his attention. It was the fact that at that first meeting, the lay leader, Cindy Davey, had brought him a quart of strawberries, fresh from her garden, and that she was known around the church as "the strawberry lady." They told stories about Cindy and how she always reaches out to visitors, people who are homebound, sick, and bereaved, by bringing them fresh strawberries. She had even been known to drop off a home-baked strawberry pie at the house of a visitor or new member.
>
> The strawberries were perfect for David's sermon. Not only did Cindy and her strawberries reveal at least one way God was present and working at Cedar Bend Church, but Cindy, by visiting people and sharing her strawberries with them, was also a model of Christian hospitality. David decided to include Cindy in his first sermon and to title it "The Gift of Strawberries."

# Help Your Spouse and Family Prepare for the Journey

Be sure to set aside time to help your spouse and children prepare for the move by visiting schools, getting information on preferred doctors, veterinarians, hairdressers, dentists, mechanics, community hobby groups or little league sports, and favored grocery stores and shopping centers. You will also want to talk to your family prior to the move about the role they wish to play in your new church. Frequently churches have expectations for the pastor's family. If your spouse is female, she may be expected to join the women's group or to help out with the children at the church. If you have children, the congregation may want them to attend church and Sunday school, and even join the youth group. If your spouse is a male, he may be asked to participate in men's groups or join the church's committees.

It is natural for a congregation to have preconceived notions of the pastor's family, but this does not mean that your spouse and children must adopt these expectations as their given roles. Your family will most likely want to be present the first Sunday to take part in the initial welcoming ceremonies, but after that, if your children are shy and don't want to join the youth group, or if your spouse wants to adopt a low profile at church, this is acceptable too. Ask your family to consider what roles they want to play, because the clearer they are with their preferences, the easier it will be for you to share this information with the church and prevent possible misunderstandings.

# Pack and Move with Your First Week in Mind

You won't want to spend your first week rummaging around in boxes looking for necessities, so consider setting aside the items you will need immediately—your robes, stoles, appropriate clothing, important books, files, reference materials, address book, and office supplies—in specially marked boxes so that you can find these items easily. One new minister was especially thankful that she had all of her clergy and funeral supplies clearly marked and positioned on the moving truck because, unfortunately, one of her new parishioners died during her move.

# Be Patient with Yourself During This Transition

Moving into a new community and becoming the pastor of a new church are both stressful events. Even though the stress may be "good stress," it is nonetheless stress. So it is essential that you take care of yourself physically, emotionally, and spiritually during this time. Be sure to schedule relaxing activities to help you and your family deal with this stress in a positive way. For example, you may want to go for a walk in the evening, have a picnic in the park, schedule a massage, or go to a movie. Some ministers like to meet with life coaches, counselors, or mentors during the first few months of their new ministry for encouragement. Local clergy groups can also be supportive. Do whatever works best for you, but don't ignore your health.

In the midst of all the necessary start-up activities, it is easy to miss the obvious: Ministry begins on day one. Enjoy these first few days as you meet the new people who will be a part of your life for the next several years, and as you begin to lay the foundations of a successful and faithful ministry.

# Pastor's Checklist

1. Can you schedule a time to talk with the previous pastor? Ask if she or he has any specific information that will help you or any thoughts or impressions that he or she wants to share. Also ask about the parsonage. Is there anything specific you need to know (e.g., when it rains the basement leaks, or certain people stop by regularly asking for assistance)?

2. Regarding the parsonage: Should the utilities be transferred into your name? What about the phone number and the listing in the phone book? Who are the service people: maintenance, repair, lawn care, and so on? What are the names of trusted neighbors?

3. Ask either the church treasurer or the chairperson of the finance committee about your pay schedule. Do you get paid monthly? Bimonthly? At the first of the month? How will you be paid? (Some churches prefer direct deposit.)

4. Will you need to provide furniture for your office? Someone on the Staff-Parish or a related committee can help you find the answer to this question.

5. Does your church have a sign or marquee? What title would you like to use? Pastor? The Reverend? Or if you have your doctorate, Dr.? Consider the implications of each title. Look around your community; what do other churches call their pastors?

6. Go over a couple of the back issues of your new church's newsletters and bulletins. How contemporary or traditional are the worship services?

7. Look through the membership directory or pictorial and begin to put names with faces. Keep a notebook of your thoughts and impressions as you begin to get to know your church's members. This can be a valuable reference for the future.

8. Does your church have a master calendar marked with the year's events? Get a copy for your files. Does your church have annual events? See if you can find out more about each event.

9. Do you have specific items for your office that will personalize it? Candy dishes filled with candy, Christian magazines on a table, photographs or artwork for the walls, copies of your favorite books

in the shelf, a dry erase board with a greeting posted on your door can help guests feel more comfortable and welcome.

10. It is a good idea to order business cards or calling cards. They are perfect for leaving in doors or at hospitals to let people know that you've stopped by for a visit. Do a search for free business cards on the Internet—several sites offer free, full-color cards. For example, www.vistaprint.com. You pay only the shipping charges.

11. Want to include a bookmark in your letter of introduction? Packages of bookmarks with Christian sayings can be purchased from a Christian bookstore or on the Internet. Some Web sites offer predesigned bookmarks that you can print for free—for example, www.vistaprint.com.

# Chapter Two

# Get Organized

**M**arjorie Lensey entered the ministry as a second career. Prior to becoming a minister, Marjorie, with her husband, Mark, had owned a restaurant that expanded into a small chain of restaurants. But while attending a weekend retreat for women who had just turned forty, Marjorie realized that, although she always felt her calling was to serve people, she now felt called to serve people with more than food. This brought Marjorie, Mark, and their thirteen-year-old daughter, Martie, to Trinity Church, where Marjorie accepted the position as their new minister.

Trinity was built in the early 1900s to serve a growing city. But as the city grew up around the church, many of its members, once residents of downtown, moved and transferred their membership to other churches. Trinity's remaining members hoped that Marjorie, having had experience as a successful restaurant owner, would help the church straighten out its finances, bring better organization to its administration, start new outreach programs, and attract new members.

As the movers unloaded the Lensey's furniture into the parsonage next door, Marjorie stood on the church's lawn and stared at the marquee that read, "Trinity welcomes new pastors: Marjorie and Mark Lensey." From behind her she heard Mark ask, "Why'd they put *my name* on that sign?"

## Be as Wise as a Serpent and as Gentle as a Lamb

Your first few months at a new church are crucial because they set the tone for your overall ministry. Even if you are shy or reserved, be sure to greet people with a smile and a firm handshake, make eye contact, listen carefully, and look for the positive in each person you meet. But be cautious until you have had plenty of time to get to know people. Sometimes parishioners come to a new minister because they have an agenda, they want to complain about past ministers, or they have control issues. Others may stop by to size you up, or to share their opinion about "what's really going on in the church." The best approach is to be polite and listen, but not accept any one person's assessment of previous ministers, other parishioners, or the church community as a whole. However, keep in mind that each person's story is important because it is one piece of the puzzle that is your church. So as you begin your new ministry, think of yourself as a detective whose job is to discover your church's:

1. *Strengths:* In what ways is this church embodying the gospel? Who are the current leaders? Which committees are the most active?
2. *Weaknesses:* With what issues is this church struggling? What committees are dysfunctional or inactive?
3. *Opportunities:* Who seems the most open to embracing the Christian life? Who is typically supportive of the pastor? Who are the potential, but currently untapped, leaders?
4. *Pitfalls:* Who is most likely to challenge the pastor? Who or what might be preventing this church from growing?

# The Key Word: Balance

During your first few months you'll be juggling several things: unpacking, getting settled, getting to know your new church and parishioners, planning services, visiting members, and meeting with the church's leadership and committees. Pace yourself. Often new ministers try to do too much in the first few months and set themselves up for burnout. To avoid this, find the right balance between your commitments to your new parish, your role as a pastor in a new community, and your obligations to your friends and family.

You may be tempted to spend all of your time doing one thing or another. For instance, you might want to spend your first week unpacking your house and settling in, or setting up your office and getting things organized at your new church. Most ministers find that a healthy balance between the two works best.

# Your First Week

Begin your first week at your office by unpacking those boxes with your essentials. Then, perhaps, some personal items, so that it doesn't seem empty. But don't be afraid to leave unpacked boxes in your office and in your house for the first few weeks. Unpacked boxes are an excellent physical reminder to your congregation that you are new and still in transition.

Be sure to keep a calendar to help you stay organized. Here are some essentials to attend to your first week:

1. The date your sermon title, Scripture verses, hymn selections, and any other items for which you are responsible are to be turned in for the bulletin; if the due day stays the same each week, jot a reminder on your calendar for at least the first few months.

2. A time when someone can meet you at the church to walk you through the service. Be sure to ask if the minister usually processes in at the beginning of the service, where to sit, where the acolytes and liturgists sit, what to expect from the choir, and if there are any objects (Bibles, flags, candlesticks, kneeling benches, flower arrangements, crosses, etc.) that have a special place on the altar, pulpit, or in the sanctuary itself. Find out where the thermostat controls are located (and, if locked, who has the key), what light switches control which lights, how to use the microphone, as well as any other audio or video equipment, and whether you are responsible for their operation before, during, or after the service.

3. Schedule time to visit any first-time visitors from the previous Sunday, and anyone who is currently in the hospital, seriously ill, or very recently bereaved. (Call and set up a time to visit instead of just popping in, until you get to know them better.)

Also look for a person or family in the church who would might act as a host family to your family the first Sunday to make sure that they find their way around, are properly introduced to people, and, if you have children, that they find the appropriate Sunday school room. This is a good way for your family to become familiar with the church and meet some of your parishioners on their own.

Sometime during your first couple of weeks, schedule a staff meeting, with both paid and volunteer staff, as well as a time to meet with the heads of committees (either individually, or if you are pressed for time or it's a small church, as a group). Consider asking each committee or staff person to write up a brief, no more than one-page, description of their committee or duties, and to make a list of their goals for the upcoming year. See if they can get this list to you the following week.

For the first few weeks, avoid making any significant changes to the church's typical routine, its newsletter or bulletin, or its worship service. Significant changes are best made once you've had a chance to get to know people and once they have had a chance to get to know you, but a small number of minor changes are fine. For example, if the previous pastor had office hours on Monday and Thursday mornings, and you want yours to be on Tuesday and Thursday afternoons, it's all right to change the days. If the pastor's day off is set on the church's calendar for Fridays, and you prefer another day, let them know this. Or if the previous pastor did not process in or out of the service, or did not offer a Gospel reading during the worship service, and these are important to you, it's okay to add the procession and reading. But be careful not to change too many things at once, and choose to make only the changes that you feel are essential. Then let the appropriate people know of the changes, clearly mark them on the bulletin, and announce them (especially if it is the addition of a reading, hymn, or prayer of the people) to avoid any confusion.

# Strategic Decisions for the Nontraditional Minister

If you are a woman, second-career minister, or a minister who is of a different race or nationality from your congregation, make appropriate decisions in the early stages of your ministry about how you want present yourself in terms of what you wear, your overall leadership style, and what role your spouse or family will play. For instance, if you are a woman who doesn't usually wear a robe or alb, but your new church has been used to seeing a male minister in a formal black robe, consider wearing a robe or alb, so that you don't unwittingly undermine your position or authority.

At Trinity, Pastor Lensey was already concerned because they had put her husband's name on their marquee, so she decided to wear business suits during the week and a black robe on Sundays. She also asked her husband to skip the first Sunday service and attend only the reception afterwards, so that the church would see her, alone, as its minister. Since Marjorie's daughter, Martie, was extremely shy and did not want to attend church until after she had the chance to meet some of the other teens on a one-to-one basis, Martie also opted to skip the first Sunday service as well as the reception.

Marjorie let the church's leadership know ahead of time that her husband and daughter would not be attending that first Sunday service, but that her husband was looking forward to meeting everyone at the reception after the service. And though she did not need to explain, she did tell the leaders about her daughter's shyness and preference to attend later.

# Your First Month

How you set your priorities for the first few months at your new church should depend upon your church's needs. For example, if the previous minister was more of an administrator and had not kept up-to-date with visiting members, consider making visiting members and forming relationships a priority. But if, like Pastor Lensey, you discover that the previous minister was known for his visits, even showing up to help celebrate birthdays and anniversaries, but wasn't a strong administrator, then without ignoring visitors or members who have special needs, you may want to start by organizing the church's records. Since Trinity specifically told Pastor Lensey that they wanted her to help get the church in order and take the lead in starting some outreach programs, she made it her priority to review the church's records, budget, and files, and to introduce herself to other ministers and community leaders.

In addition to setting priorities:

- Familiarize yourself with the church's calendar for the entire year (and coordinate it with your own), taking note of days your congregation has marked, as well as the dates that outside groups regularly use the church, such as Boy or Girl Scout troops, programs for mothers, AA groups, and so on.
- Keep handy a list of the addresses, names, and phone numbers of local shelters (noting which ones accept women and children), advocacy centers, food pantries, bus stations, low-cost daycare centers, Head Start programs, and nearby grocery stores that accept food vouchers.
- Set up a regular visitation schedule. Pastors find it helpful to have one list organized either alphabetically or by regions, and another organized by categories: members who are homebound, inactive members, new members, members who have recently returned to or recently left the church, members in nursing homes or hospitals, and members who are newly bereaved. You can't visit everyone in your first month, but do visit as many as possible and keep a personal record of the time and date of each visit, and any other notations that you find informative.
- Take the time to get to know any staff (paid or volunteer), as well as the church's leadership and the church's guardians (those matriarchs and patriarchs of the church who may or may not serve in official leadership positions). Make it a priority to form relationships with these members.
- Review the church's budget (including the budget for the pastor), Sunday school materials, minutes from past meetings (paying special attention to the committee that oversees the staff, the parish, and

the church's finances), the church's hymnal or list of songs they typically sing (and which ones they like the best), past newsletters, bulletins (particularly for special services), and any previous advertisements.

- Organize a plan to recognize members on their birthdays and on other special days, such as significant anniversaries (wedding, death of a loved one, or their baptism). Doing something as simple as sending a postcard or note, or making a phone call on important days, will help you build a stronger relationship with your members. This correspondence can be prepared in advance, then mailed just prior to the appropriate date.
- Note in your address book the name and number of the flower shop your church uses. Often churches will have an account with one or two flower shops in town.
- Obtain a copy (or make sure there is a copy on file) of your church's tax exempt number, as well as copies of any reimbursement forms you will need to fill out to get reimbursed for your expenses.
- Make a list of the funeral homes that your church's members frequently use. Stop by and introduce yourself to the owners.
- Find out which hospitals are nearby. Clergy can sign up at most hospitals for a clergy parking permit. In an emergency, these are handy.
- Familiarize yourself with the bulk mailing services your church uses to send out newsletters or other notices. It is helpful if a pastor understands how to use this service, should he or she want to send out letters or other mailings to everyone in the congregation.
- Make sure that you monitor your stress level and take adequate care of yourself and your family. Don't neglect spouses, children, or pets. Remember, they are adjusting too.

# Make Important Decisions about Leadership

Pastors often hear the advice: "Don't change anything or start any new programs within the first six months." But no one rule applies to all situations. The best approach is to take the first few months of your ministry to learn everything you can about your congregation so that you can responsibly decide what type of leadership is best for your particular church. Making an uninformed decision about leadership style or too many significant changes can kill a new ministry before it begins. So before you change things, start new programs, take a stand on issues, or make any one program or idea your priority, it is essential that you know your congregation's overall health, needs, commitment, and context:

1. **Is your church healthy?** Does the congregation have a clear sense of identity and vision, or are they struggling to define themselves? If they do have an identity, what is it and do you think it is accurate? Do the members have confidence in their pastor, or have previous pastors left them hurting or divided? Do they treat each other with respect and work well together to solve problems, or is there a high level of internal conflict and chaos? What changes have they made in the past ten years and how were these changes received? How are guests or new members welcomed? Do visitors come back after their initial visit? Do members stay, or do they stay for less than five years and then leave? Would you recommend this church to someone in crisis or in need?

2. **What are your church's current needs?** Are they in the midst of making a decision on an important issue? What is the average age of the members, and has the overall membership grown or declined in the past ten years? How are their finances? Do committees meet on a regular basis? What opportunities are there for fellowship, study, and spiritual growth? What outreach programs does this church offer?

3. **What is the current commitment level of its members?** How many members actively support the church's programs? Are volunteers plentiful or in short supply? How many members tithe regularly? Does this church spend too much or too little time and money on building maintenance? How many members would sign up to serve dinner at a homeless shelter? Which event would have greater attendance, a church bazaar or a Christmas Eve service?

4. **What is the church's context?** Is this a rural, urban, or suburban church? What is going on within a five-mile radius of your church? What is nearby? Is there a library? Mall? What other churches are in this area? Is this area growing and developing? Run-down and dying? In a period of renewal? What is the overall economic status? What is the housing like? Mostly single family homes? Multiple family dwellings? Is this a multi-cultural area or a predominantly ethnic neighborhood? Politically, would you say this area is liberal or conservative? Is your church liberal or conservative?

If you discover that your church is mostly healthy, has confidence in its pastor, and its commitment level is high, then it may be acceptable to consider some new ideas, make changes, or add new programs within the first six months of your ministry if, and only if, the changes or programs fit well with your church's needs, its commitment level, and its context. If you discover that your church is not healthy, does not have confidence in its pastor, or has a low commitment level, work to improve these areas before sharing your ideas, making changes, or starting new programs.

# Record Keeping

In many ways, serving as a pastor of a church is like running a business. In addition to preaching the gospel and consoling the grieving, the pastor is called to be an administrator. Since Marjorie Lensey already had experience running a restaurant, administrator was a comfortable role for her at Trinity. But if record keeping doesn't come easily for you, take care not to get behind on the administrative tasks.

Trinity's church records had not been updated in several years. So her first week, Pastor Lensey worked with Diane, the part-time secretary, to review the membership records and mark each member's current status.

In terms of records, at a minimum keep the following sets and have them easily accessible:

1.  *Personal Pastoral Record:* This record is yours and will travel with you throughout your life. Bound books especially for this purpose can be purchased at church supply stores. Subdivide this record into sections: baptisms, confirmations, weddings, and funerals.

2.  *Local Church Record:* This is the church's record of baptisms, confirmations, weddings, funerals, and the official membership list of current and former members. Be sure to familiarize yourself with how these records are kept and whether or not it is your responsibility to keep them. Most churches keep an official hard copy of this record but, in addition to the hard copy, hopefully they will also have a computer database of members. If your church doesn't have a computer database of its members, this would be a good long-term goal, because electronic databases are invaluable for maintaining up-to-date records of constantly changing addresses, phone numbers, and e-mail addresses.

3.  *Working Membership Record:* This is your personal record of the church's members with their addresses, phone numbers, and e-mail addresses. As members join, leave, or die during the year, make a note of this in the margins. Don't simply reprint this list, because you can use the annotated list when you fill out your end-of-the-year reports. Your personal notes in the margins will help you keep track of your visits, phone calls, letters, and any important details: Jane

Doe is ill with cancer, John Smith lost his wife last year, and so on. If needed, more detailed records of your visits can be kept on separate note cards. Put a star next to the names of members who need special attention, then frequently review your contact with them.

4. *Calendar:* As mentioned earlier, a calendar is essential, not only because you'll be juggling a variety of important tasks, but also because you can use it as a record of how you spend your time. A record of your time is important for two reasons: to periodically check and see if the balance between administrative duties, pastoral visits, and worship preparation is as it should be, and, should anyone in the congregation question how you spend your time, you will have an answer in the form of a documented record.

# Money Management

In addition to being an administrator, the pastor also acts as the chief executive officer in the church. It is the pastor's responsibility to know how much money and other assets, such as stocks and bonds, the church has and who has control over their expenditure. But one note of caution: The pastor should never write his or her own checks for salary or reimbursement. In fact all financial transactions should be cosigned by at least one church member and never solely by the pastor. Occasionally obtain and review a copy of:

1. *All of the church's financial accounts.* This would be a list of its operating budget and every one of its accounts: both those actually tied to the budget and any separate accounts the church has that are not a formal part of the budget. Some churches keep separate accounts for women's groups, youth groups, or special projects, such as a building fund or a memorial account. Find out who writes the checks for all of the church's accounts. Despite whatever separate accounts exist, ask if there is one treasurer, or do different members have direct access to different accounts? As pastor, it is not your responsibility to keep these records, and in fact in most denominations the pastor should not be the one maintaining these records, but make sure you receive regular statements from the appropriate financial officers, at least quarterly.

2. *All sources of church income.* Be aware of how your church is supporting itself. In addition to the traditional sources of income, find out if there are other sources of income, such as an annual church hot dog stand at the county fair or a set of stocks that pay twice-annual dividends. Ask too if the church has a standard fee for outside groups

who wish to use the sanctuary or the fellowship hall, perhaps for a wedding or a reception. Finally, look at the relationship between the worship offerings and the church's expenses. Is the church holding steady or, like so many churches, is there a large gap between the monthly offerings and the monthly expenses?

3. *The record of individual giving.* Although some pastors prefer not to know what individual members tithe because it might bias how they treat that member, a strong case can also be made for occasionally reviewing this record. Early signs of conflict or discontentment with the church, personal problems, or family problems frequently show up as decreased giving to the church, and these are important matters of which the pastor should be aware. Also, the pastor should acknowledge with a sincere thank-you dramatic increases in giving, not just from wealthy members, but also from people who are struggling.

# How to Get Reimbursed for Your Expenses

Most churches have a reimbursement policy in place for pastors. If your church does not have such a policy, consider asking them to pass one. For example:

> The pastor will be reimbursed for ordinary and necessary business expenses incurred in the performance of pastoral duties when he or she submits a reimbursement request that substantiates the amount, date, purpose, and place of the expense. (Original receipts must be provided for expenses over $75. The pastor should keep copies for his or her personal records.) The request will be submitted to the church treasurer (or other designated person/committee for approval) within sixty days of the expense, and any excess amounts received will be returned within one hundred and twenty days of receipt. The church will not report properly reimbursed, substantiated payments as income.

If your church *has* passed such a policy, then budgetary items for the pastor such as travel, continuing education, and miscellaneous pastoral expenses can be added to the church budget. Whenever an expense occurs, the pastor can pay for it and get reimbursed later or let the church be billed directly, but in either case these expenses are *not* to be reported to the IRS as income because they are church funds and not part of the pastor's salary. Any expense that is directly related to the local church's unique mission, and is not a private, personal expense of the pastor, is an appropriate item for reimbursement.

Keep a business reimbursement record for all of your funds, subdivided into the appropriate categories. For example, in addition to business expenses, if your church has a pastor's discretionary fund, money set aside that can be used to help individuals who come to the church needing assistance, or a budget line for the youth group, keep separate records of how you use each of these funds. Regarding travel, be sure to maintain a log of your mileage, recording destination, purpose, miles traveled, and date. (Pastoral visits can simply be marked "confidential pastoral visit.")

# Housing Allowance

One of the more confusing topics for most new clergy is taxes. Be sure to consult the latest IRS publications for the specifics and the latest changes, but in general, clergy are *not required* to pay income tax on the cost of maintaining their homes, although they *are required* to pay Social Security/self-employment tax on this cost. So, for example, if clergy own or rent their own homes, they *can exclude* the cost of maintaining their home from their income. (Churches should declare a portion of the pastor's salary as a housing allowance, and then this amount is not required to be reported as income.) But if a parsonage is provided by the church, clergy are required to *add in* the fair rental value of the parsonage when paying their Social Security/self-employment tax.

# Taking Vacations

Within the first three months at your church, decide when you want to take your vacation for the upcoming year. Go ahead and pick the dates and set them aside because you will need to find a substitute preacher and liturgist if a Sunday is involved, and because if you do not set your vacation early, you run the risk of the church scheduling "must-attend events" throughout the year, making it difficult for you to take your vacation.

Check with the appropriate Staff-Parish chairperson or denominational official to ask if there is an established vacation policy for pastors. Two to four weeks, with two to four Sundays off, is typical. Let the church's leadership know well in advance when you have scheduled any vacation time and be sure to leave a contact number with them to use in case of emergencies. Usually this will be the phone number of the lay leader or a clergy colleague in town, who in turn will have contact information where you can be reached.

In addition to vacation time, pastors have a good degree of flexibility in the ordering of their week, but they are also on call 24/7 for emergencies, so make sure that you set aside regular time off. One full day off a week is standard. This day should be the same day each week so that it can be announced to the congregation, included in your formal schedule (in addition to your office hours), and perhaps printed in the church's newsletter. Make it clear that on this day you are not to be disturbed unless there is a true emergency.

# Pastor's Checklist

1. Local church ministry is one of the most meaningful and enjoyable vocations, but it can also be one of the most stressful. A good rule for pastors is to keep track of hours and to try to maintain—on average—a fifty- to fifty-five-hour workweek. This means five ten-hour days, plus at least five hours on Sunday.
2. Schedule time each week to care for your mind, body, and soul. Spend time with your family, but also take time for personal hobbies, entertainment, exercise, proper nutrition, and relationships. Consider meetings with a professional, such as a life coach, mentor, counselor, or spiritual director, as this can also help keep burnout at bay.
3. To refresh your soul and reenergize your ministry, set aside a few days each month for prayer, reflection, or study. Spiritual retreat centers offer everything from spiritual direction (where an experienced guide helps you discern God's presence and will in your life), to guided and private retreats, to professional and personal development seminars, to special events and workshops dealing with the spiritual life. Look for a spiritual guide or retreat center in your area, or contact Spiritual Directors International: P.O. Box 3584, Bellevue, WA 98009. (425) 455-1565, www.sdiworld.org.
4. Most pastors take part in continuing education events. This is not vacation time, so let the church leaders know if a continuing education class or retreat will take you out of town overnight. Some churches also set aside funds to assist with these expenses, so check with your finance chairperson. Many denominations offer regular continuing education retreats, and Fred Pryor Seminars CareerTrack is one of the largest national continuing education companies. Their one-day seminars (offered nationwide) provide professional training on many subjects such as conflict and stress management, communication skills, personal growth, time management, and more. For more information call 1-800-780-8476, or stop by their Web site: www.pryor.com.

# CHAPTER THREE

# LEAD THE WORSHIP SERVICE

As Leo Douglas climbed into the pulpit his first Sunday, his heart was beating a mile a minute. He took a deep breath and with the words "Good morning," he began his service at Christ Memorial Church. Pastor Douglas had already met with the leadership the previous week, and together they had planned the welcoming ceremony. (*The United Methodist Book of Worship* contains a sample induction ceremony. See the Pastor's Checklist for more information.) He had also let the worship committee select the music and print the bulletins, so that he could focus on the Scripture lessons and the sermon for the day.

Pastor Douglas wanted to make a good first impression, so he had been busy working behind the scenes to make his first Sunday look effortless. He had practiced his sermon in the empty sanctuary the night before, and had placed a copy of the sermon, along with a glass of water and a watch, on the pulpit. And knowing that he'd be nervous, he had written out the Lord's Prayer and had placed it where he could see it, even though he had prayed it countless times before from memory.

Taking his mentor's advice—come early, leave late—Leo was the first person to arrive at the church that Sunday, and was well prepared, rested, fed, and ready to meet his new congregation. Although he had been tempted to hide out in his new office until the service started, he knew that it was better to walk around and make himself visible. So he briefly visited some of the Sunday school classes and greeted people in the halls until about fifteen minutes before the service. Then he retreated to his office, collected his thoughts, said a prayer, and put on his robe.

With only a few minor glitches, his first service went well, though there was one startling moment. About halfway through his sermon Leo realized that he had locked one of his legs, and when he went to unlock it, it had fallen asleep and he almost collapsed. But he quickly recovered and forged ahead.

After the service, Leo stayed and greeted each one of his members. By the end of the morning he was exhausted, but pleased with how things had gone. It was not until he started to drive home that he realized, "Oh no, I have to do this all over again next week!"

# The Pastor as Worship Leader

As pastor, leading the worship service is your most visible and perhaps most important activity: you set the order and style of worship, organize the worship assistants, attend to the musical and visual elements of the service, provide the primary message each week, lead the congregation in prayer, and preside over Holy Communion. Perhaps more vital still, you serve as symbol—a holy presence. Your primary goal is to direct the congregation's attention to God.

# Dress Appropriately

Make good choices in terms of what you wear. If your denomination has specific standards for dress, then the choice is easy, but many churches allow for a variety of options:

1. The alb (white robe, with or without a hood) is for pastors who want to emphasize the sacramental ministry of Holy Communion.
2. The formal, academic gown (black robe) is suitable for pastors who want to accent the preaching of God's Word.
3. The clergy shirt with clerical collar can be worn alone or under an alb or gown. A clergy shirt is particularly useful during services such as weddings and funerals, it quickly identifies you as the minister.
4. Contemporary dress can be worn by pastors seeking to emphasize the priesthood of all believers.
5. A liturgical cross on a chain or cord, or a stole draped around your shoulders, can help identify you as the pastor and also symbolically point to God, no matter what type of dress you choose. Your stole can be coordinated with the coverings on the altar and pulpit: purple or blue for preparatory seasons such as Advent and Lent, white and gold for Christmas and Easter, bright red for Pentecost, green for ordinary time after Epiphany and Pentecost, and white for weddings and funerals.

If you do choose a contemporary style of dress, dark or neutral solid colors are best. Bright colors or bold patterns can be distracting. For men, a suit works well, as do dress pants and a dress shirt with or without a tie. For women, a skirt or pant suit is appropriate, but be careful about skirt length and heel height—short skirts and high heels can be both awkward and uncomfortable. If you are unsure of what to wear, find out how past pastors have dressed and pay attention to how your congregation dresses too. But remember, even if your congregation is made up of people who wear jeans and casual dress to church, sometimes they still expect to see the pastor in a suit, robe, or alb.

# The Worship Service

There are three aspects to a worship service: the order, the style, and its overall theme. While the theme of the service (or its primary subject and focus) will change each week, the order and style generally remain the same.

Most congregations will be expecting some changes in the worship service from a new pastor, but remember, multiple changes all at once can disorient a congregation. Therefore, it is best to avoid changing too much of the worship service until the congregation has learned to trust you, and until you have had the chance to identify the important rituals that define the church as a community. For example, there may be special songs that they sing each Sunday, a particular greeting time in the service that they value, or a popular time with children to which they look forward. Familiarize yourself with your church's rituals before you change or remove anything from the service. And always consult your worship committee or governing board before making significant changes or altering the basic order or style of worship.

In terms of changes, don't make them arbitrarily. Instead, look at the overall service and ask: Does the order and style of the service fit well with my church's context, mission, and vision? What about the music? Does it match the context, mission, and vision too? Do any of the elements seem awkward or out of place? What about the transitions between the different elements of the service? Are they smooth or distracting?

# The Order of Worship

Just as a movie is made of many scenes that, combined, tell a single story, a worship service is also made of a number of liturgical acts, or scenes, that combine to form a structure in which people can worship God. It is the pastor's responsibility to make sure that the hymns, prayers, readings, sermon, offering, and other acts all transition easily from one to the next and that there is an underlying logic to this order. Although there are many variations, the three most common orders of worship are outlined below.

## A Service Emphasizing the Word (Preaching)

This structure has most of the prayers and hymns near the beginning of the service, prior to the offering and sermon. It builds toward and emphasizes the sermon, which is at the end.

Gathering:
    Prelude
    Call to Worship
    Opening Hymn
Time of Prayer:
    Opening Prayer
    Confession
    Lord's Prayer
    Act of Praise / Hymn
Proclamation of the Word:
    Scripture Lessons
    Affirmation of Faith
    Pastoral Prayer
    Offering
    Hymn
    Sermon
    Invitation to Christian Discipleship
    Closing Hymn
    Benediction

Some disadvantages of this order are that the Scripture readings can get lost among the prayers and hymns, and that it does not provide a place for Holy Communion. But the advantage is that the congregation leaves the service having just heard the main message for the day.

## A Service Emphasizing Word and Table (Preaching and Communion)

This structure divides into two parts: the Service of the Word (preaching) and the Service of the Table (Holy Communion).

Gathering:
  Prelude
  Call to Worship
  Opening Hymn
  Opening Prayer(s)
Proclamation of the Word:
  Scripture Lessons
  Sermon
Responses to the Word:
  Affirmations of Faith
  Prayers of Confession
  Pastoral Prayer or Prayers of the People
  Offering
Service of Thanksgiving:
  Holy Communion or, alternatively, a Prayer of Thanksgiving and the Lord's
    Prayer
  Closing Hymn
  Benediction

A disadvantage of this structure is that it is not as powerful on Sundays when Holy Communion is not celebrated. However, the advantage is that it gives people a chance to respond to hearing God's Word with their offerings and prayers.

## The Praise Service (Traditional or Contemporary)

A Praise Service has a less formal structure, and it may or may not have its particular order printed in a bulletin. As the name indicates, the focus is on praising God, especially through song, rather than on the traditionally ordered liturgical acts.

This service begins with either traditional hymns or more contemporary songs. In addition to congregational singing, special musical presentations can be scheduled, perhaps with testimonial introductions by the performers or liturgical dancers. As the singing draws to a close, the songs typically grow slower in tempo and quieter in tone, in order to prepare the congregation for a time of prayer.

Singing
Prayers: Pastoral, Extemporaneous, or Silent Prayer
Scripture Reading
Theatrical Dramas (optional)
Extended Sermon or Message
Offering

An Altar Call (optional)
An Anointing with Oil or Laying on of Hands (optional)
Holy Communion (optional)

The disadvantage of this service is that with praise being the primary focus, other aspects of worship tend to be neglected: prayers of confession, creeds, hymns with theological topics, and so on, all of which serve to invite Christians to deepen their faith and their relationship with God.

But the strength of the praise service is its adaptability. For example, it can be used in large or small settings and can be contemporary or traditional in tone, or a mix of both. When special elements, such as a band, or a drama are added, the service can be held in an auditorium with five hundred people, or when the singing and the sermon are shortened, and the offering omitted, the praise service works well for an evening chapel service with as little as three people. If Holy Communion is removed, it can also serve as a "seeker service," where the songs and sermon serve to introduce an "unchurched" audience to the Christian message.

# Style Matters in Worship

During worship, people will watch you and follow your lead, so pay attention to your gestures: keep your hands folded in front of you or carry a book during processions, acknowledge the altar as you pass by it, and make eye contact with the congregation when you are preaching.

There is no right and wrong when it comes to overall style, but it is an issue in many churches. Things such as age, background, race and ethnicity of parishioners, and whether or not the church is rural or urban, or conservative or liberal, can determine how formal or informal a church's style is. In order to meet the needs of different people, some churches offer two services: one traditional and the other contemporary. Traditional approaches rely upon preprinted bulletins or books of worship, piano or organ music for hymns, the pastor standing at a pulpit to preach, and formal liturgical acts, such as professions of faith and corporate prayers. On the other hand, contemporary services employ overhead projectors, CD players, Power Point demonstrations, contemporary music, extemporaneous prayers, and unscripted sermons.

If your church is large enough to accommodate two services, then this may be an option, but if it is not, another solution is a *blended worship* that uses a combination of traditional and contemporary elements, especially in terms of music. The advantage of a blended worship is that it brings the entire congregation, in all of its diversity, together in corporate worship, and celebrates that diversity. Church members, no matter how traditional or contemporary, are usually willing to compromise some of their personal preferences so that everyone can share in worship together.

In terms of a blended service, keep in mind that contemporary praise songs work best at the beginning of a service, while slower, more prayerful songs, either traditional, contemporary, or songs such as the elegant chants from France's Taizé community, are a better choice for the offering or for prayer. Because of their theological depth, many of the traditional hymns work best after a sermon. Their refrains can also serve as transitions between the different acts or scenes in the service, such as the transition between the opening gathering and the reading of Scripture.

If your church is not currently using a blended style, do your homework before introducing this style. You will want to make sure that you have the support of the church's leadership and guardians, and that you give anyone who is resistant the chance to adjust to possible changes. Even if you feel that it is the right time to introduce a blended service, keep the changes to a minimum at first. Never change both the order of worship and the style at the same time. Also, take care to make sure that the service keeps a central theme and focus, even if the style may be "blended."

# Worship Assistants

Besides the pastor, who usually takes part in the worship service at your church? Do members of the congregation offer special music, or serve as greeters, readers, acolytes, ushers, or communion stewards? The more the pastor shares the responsibility of leading worship, the more the members of the church feel that the worship service is truly *their* service, and that they are not simply an audience.

Your church may have worship assistants, liturgists, musicians, and acolytes already in place, but if not, volunteers can be recruited by sending around sign-up sheets and by asking your leadership for the names of possible volunteers. If your church does have assistants, make sure to include these people in worship regularly. In addition to the roles already mentioned, members can take part in the worship service by copying and folding bulletins, arranging for altar flowers and candles, being responsible for the communion bread and wine, decorating for the holidays, making banners to hang in the sanctuary, and setting up microphones and managing any audio or video equipment.

# The Musical Element of Worship

In addition to worship assistants, musicians are invaluable for worship. However, if live music is unavailable, recorded music works well too. Prerecorded collections of praise songs, Taizé music, and hymnal music with organ or piano accompaniment are available for purchase (see "Pastor's Checklist").

If you do have members involved in music ministry, meet with them to familiarize yourself with how the music is coordinated. It is also helpful to identify with which songs are familiar to the congregation and which are their favorites. One way to do this is to review past bulletins and make a list of hymns used. But an even better way is to ask members of your congregation who have been involved in selecting the music for worship to put together a list of, or to put an asterisk in their hymnals (in pencil) next to, those songs they think the congregation knows well enough to sing, and a star next to those that are particular favorites. Compare hymnals, then mark your own hymnal with the selections. As you use the songs in worship, note the date when the song was used in your hymnal and make it a priority to use at least one familiar hymn at each service and a variety of the members' favorites over time.

Find out too if there are any special rituals in terms of music. For example, a church may expect a certain member's grandson to play saxophone each Christmas, or another member to sing a solo at Easter, yet they may still want a special invitation from the pastor.

Finally, ask the congregation for the names of anyone who has special musical ability, either as a vocalist or instrumentalist, who may not have been previously invited to take part in a worship service. Invite them to participate. Remember, a member need not be a musician of a professional quality to share their talent with your church and with God.

# Preaching

While some pastors prepare one sermon per week, others prepare sermons in groups, usually grouping no more than five or six Sundays together at a time, for example, the four Sundays of Advent or the six of Lent. Let's turn again to Pastor Leo Douglas from the beginning of the chapter to illustrate how this works.

After his first month at Christ Memorial, Pastor Douglas found himself overwhelmed by the process of having to prepare a sermon and order a worship service each week. So on the advice of a colleague, he decided to group his Sundays together and prepare four services at a time. But to do this he first had to make a decision: Did he want to follow the lectionary for the liturgical year, or did he want to plan a series of sermons for each month that either highlighted a biblical character (such as Moses or David), highlighted a particular story in the Bible (such as the miracles that Jesus performed), or that focused on a certain aspect of the Christian life (some pastors do a series on prayer, fasting, service, tithing, forgiveness, and other such topics)?

Pastor Douglas decided that it would be best to follow the lectionary—the three-year cycle of assigned Scripture readings for each Sunday—because it provided a well-organized selection already coordinated to the church year and made a whole range of lectionary worship aids available to him, including prewritten prayers and musical suggestions. Following the lectionary also allowed him to discuss sermon ideas with some of his colleagues who also used it.

# Creative Ideas and Structures for Sermons

There are countless ways to structure a sermon so that your messages stay fresh, unique, and interesting. Many books, newsletters, and online services also offer creative ideas and illustrations for sermons. A wise preacher will, over time, read collections of contemporary sermons and experiment with a variety of different forms (see "Pastor's Checklist"). Here are a few structures that many preachers find useful:

1. *The Theatrical Approach.* The pastor takes on the persona of one of the characters from the Bible and retells the events of the story from that character's perspective. For example, one might tell the story of Jesus' crucifixion from the perspective of the thief on the cross: you are the thief being taken from the cell, dragged down the street, beaten, and then nailed to a cross. As the thief, share your thoughts and feelings, what you see and hear, your initial perspective of Jesus hanging beside you, then reveal how you realize that there is something deeper, more profound taking place. A similar sermon could be told from the perspective of one of the Roman guards or other witnesses.
2. *The Guessing Game.* Present the congregation with a question, for example, "Where is heaven?" Then offer possible answers, some fanciful ones, like heaven being a planet beyond Pluto, and some that are partially true, like heaven being an experience of the heart. Your goal here is to take your congregation on a thoughtful journey to consider what and where heaven really is, by helping them to discern what heaven is and what it is not, where it is and where it is not, and to put aside any ill-conceived notions of heaven.
3. *The Lecture.* In this structure, the pastor is a teacher, teaching the congregation a particular idea or lesson from the Christian story, so the organizational pattern is a logical one. For example, present a thesis such as, true happiness is found in God's will, then go on to explain why this is true. Next offer a second thesis—God's will is made known to us in Christ—and explain this as well. Then offer a

possible conclusion to suggest how all of this is still relevant today—Christ is made known through the church, which is why what we do in churches today is so important.

4. *The Jewel.* A particular theme is chosen and explored from various different angles. With this style, it is appropriate to tell contemporary and, perhaps, even personal stories. For example, if the day's Scripture is the one where Jesus talks about his true family, one might take as the theme, the word *home*: Where is home? What is home? The sermon could then be designed around two or three stories that explore *home* from different angles. For example, Pastor Douglas might want to start with a story about the time he got lost, separated from his mother, in a grocery store as a child, and how he feared he might never see his mother or his home again. Then he could compare that story with the story of a young refugee who travels from camp to camp looking for his mother, but with the odds against him that he will ever find her or be able to return home. Finally, Pastor Douglas could talk about what Jesus meant by *home*, and how as Christians though we are sometimes lost, we are never alone or homeless. The point with the jewel sermon is not so much a logical one, but rather the goal is to offer an insight, something that reveals the deeper significance of the day's biblical passage.

In terms of delivery, some preachers like to preach from manuscripts, some from notes or an outline, while others choose to memorize their sermons. Do what is most comfortable for you, but regardless, be sure to prepare thoroughly. It is imperative for preachers who do not use a manuscript to know what they are going to say ahead of time, so they don't ramble. Preachers who do use a manuscript must still be familiar with it so that they can make eye contact and engage their audience.

One of the benefits of preaching from an outline, manuscript, or notes, is that this provides you with a hard copy of your sermon that can be saved for future reference, then revised and preached again at your next church. It is also a good idea to make a title page for each sermon with its text, topic, theme, and title, along with the secular and liturgical date it was first preached listed at the top of the page. This cover page can serve as an aid for you as you arrange the rest of your service around your sermon's main theme.

# Sermon Delivery

One of the biggest mistakes new preachers make is that they speak too fast. This is why many preachers, new and not-so-new alike, like to practice their sermons out loud or even record themselves preaching the sermon prior to the Sunday service. As a preacher, or orator, your voice is your instrument. Pay attention to intonation (the tone and inflection you use), volume (while you always want to be loud enough to be heard, using different tones can help emphasize different points), and energy level (sermons delivered without enthusiasm or vigor can become boring).

# Holy Communion

Although the essentials of communion remain the same across denominational lines—a thanksgiving prayer to God in which Jesus' Last Supper is recalled and the Holy Spirit is invoked to bless the bread and cup—the particulars vary. Check with your worship leaders to find out what the customs are in your new church, and be sure to work out the specifics well in advance of the service. Some questions to ask are:

- How often do members receive Holy Communion?
- What sort of bread is used (wafers, pita, leaven loaves)?
- What sort of wine is used (alcoholic, nonalcoholic, grape juice)?
- Who is responsible for setting up this service (you, someone in the church)?
- Will the plate and cup be up front at the beginning of the service, or will they be brought forward by the ushers during the offering?
- How will the congregation receive (kneeling at the altar, forming a single line)?
- Who will assist you with the cup(s)?
- Will the congregation drink from the cup or dip the bread into the cup?
- What happens to the leftover bread and wine (eaten by pastor, poured in church garden)?

# Children and Worship

Does your church have rituals and practices in place in terms of ministering to children? If yes, stick with these, at least until you have had a chance to meet with the parents who regularly attend to see if they are happy with the current system. If your church does not have anything in place for the children, a meeting with the parents and church leaders will be necessary to discuss the options, which can include:

1. Sunday school for children or a children's worship service (or some combination of the two) that takes place at the same time as the adult worship, but separately. (The adults go to worship while the children go to the children's program.)
2. Children attend the worship with their parents—with or without a special children's sermon or time for children during the service. The children then attend Sunday school before or after the service.
3. Children attend the service up through the children's sermon after the Gospel reading, at which time they are dismissed for an activity time elsewhere in the church.

What you decide will depend upon your church's resources (especially volunteer resources), combined with the desires of the members and parents. But whatever you decide, remember it is a good idea to include children in the Sunday service (even if only occasionally) by having them sing a special song, offer a special program, or serve as acolytes. Older children and teenagers can also assist as ushers, greeters, Scripture readers, and communion assistants.

# Pastor's Checklist

## *Liturgical Aids*

*The United Methodist Book of Worship.* Nashville: United Methodist Publishing House, 1992.

This book is useful for the variety of prayers that it offers. It is also useful for the special services it includes: a Christmas Lessons and Carols Service, an Ash Wednesday Service, the Tenebrae Service (Service of Shadows) for Holy Thursday, the Easter Vigil, a Love Feast (which is particularly appropriate around Thanksgiving), among others. Finally, it includes the order of worship for the induction of a new minister.

*Book of Common Worship* (Louisville: Westminster/John Knox Press, 1993).

Provides orders of worship and liturgical texts for each Sunday and for every festival and season throughout the year. It is also available in a CD-ROM edition.

Colbert S. Cartwright and O.I. Cricket Harrison, eds. *Chalice Worship* (St. Louis: Chalice Press, 1997).

Provides 132 complete services and more than 900 individual worship resources.

Hoyt L. Hickman, et. al. *Handbook of the Christian Year*. Nashville: Abingdon Press, 1986.
As the title suggests, this handbook helps the minister prepare the church for the various Christian seasons.

Michael J. O'Donnell. *Lift Up Your Hearts: Years A, B, and C*, revised and expanded. Akron, Ohio: OSL Publications, 1996.
This book provides communion prayers coordinated to each Sunday of the three-year lectionary cycle.

Igniting Worship Series from Abingdon Press.
This series provides sermon outlines, calls to worship, prayers, and benedictions.

*The Abingdon Worship Annual* by Abingdon Press.
Provides resources for traditional and contemporary services with calls to worship, invocations, prayers, and benedictions for each Sunday of the Year. It also includes resources for Christmas Eve, other holy days, and special occasions.

See www.WorshipConnection.com for additional liturgy resources.

## Preaching Aids

Fred B. Craddock. *Preaching*. Nashville: Abingdon Press, 1985.

Fred B. Craddock, John H. Hayes, Carl R. Holladay, and Gene M. Tucker. *Preaching the New Common Lectionary*. Nashville: Abingdon Press, 1986.

*The Abingdon Preaching Annual*, edited by David N. Mosser.
This comes in both print and CD.

Kirk Byron Jones. *The Jazz of Preaching: How to Preach with Great Freedom and Joy*. Nashville: Abingdon Press, 2004.

Teresa Fry Brown. *Weary Throats and New Songs: Black Women Proclaiming God's Word*. Nashville: Abingdon Press, 2003.

The Web sites www.lectionary.org and www.SermonWriter.com also offer exegetical and preaching aids.

# Musical Aids

*The United Methodist Hymnal* on CD.

An excellent resource if your church does not have a regular pianist or organist. This multivolume collection provides organ music for every hymn in the *United Methodist Hymnal*.

Various praise songs and Taizé chants are available on CD from www.amazon.com and other sites.

# Worship Planning Worksheet

Secular Date _____ Liturgical Date _____ Liturgical Color: _____
Special Emphasis (e.g., a holiday or youth Sunday)? _____
Communion? _____ If yes, who is to assist? _____

## Scripture:
First Reading _____
Psalm or Response _____
Second Reading _____
Gospel Reading _____
Sermon Theme _____

## Congregational Hymns:
First _____
Second _____
Third _____
Other? _____

## Other Music:
Before Scripture _____
During Prayer _____
At Offering _____
Anthems or Special Music _____
Other Service Music (prelude, postlude, communion) _____
_____
_____

## Worship Assistants:
Greeters _____
Acolytes _____
Liturgists/Readers _____
Children's Sermon _____
Other (Ushers, etc.) _____

## Visuals or Special Arrangements:
_____
_____
_____

# Chapter Four

# Conduct Weddings and Funerals

As a newly licensed pastor, Michelle Winter looked forward to conducting weddings, and in a sense, even funerals in her new church. Obviously she didn't want anyone to die, but she considered it a most precious privilege of ministry to be invited into people's lives during moments of great joy or sadness. Like many new ministers, Michelle felt she was well prepared for such services because she had assisted at funerals before, and she had attended many weddings as a guest. But it wasn't until her first wedding and funeral that she realized the true amount of preparation involved.

## Setting a Wedding Policy

Pastors represent both the church and the state at weddings. Regarding your civil recognition as an agent of the state, contact the clerk of courts to find out the requirements in your state before you perform your first wedding: sometimes civil recognition is automatic for ordained and licensed ministers, but in other states you need to fill out and file a form with the court.

Regarding your role as representative of the church, your presence is not only a sign of your personal support for the marriage, it is a sign of the church's support as well and indicates that the marriage is to be a Christian marriage. Therefore it is important to decide ahead of time what type of weddings you can perform with integrity, because there will be a variety of people asking you to officiate at their weddings. Sometimes the answer is obvious. For example, Pastor Michelle Winter easily said no to the anonymous couple who called on

December 20 wanting to get married on Christmas Day. But she readily agreed to marry the young, active couple from her church who approached her nine months ahead of time. At other times, however, the answer is more ambiguous:

1. What do you say to an active member's son who has not been to church in years and has repeatedly stated that he has no interest in church and does not plan to return?

To this request Pastor Winter, as a courtesy to the parents, agreed to perform the service—but only at a place outside the church, such as a private home or rented hall. She also removed the Christian blessing at the end because she did not feel comfortable serving as the church's representative, given the groom's feelings toward the church.

2. What do you do with the moderately active couple in your church who have been dating only a short time when they spontaneously decide that they want to get married next week, and so don't have time for any premarital counseling?

Pastor Winter required at least three and usually four counseling sessions prior to the service, which in practical terms meant at least one month's notification before the wedding date, although her preference was three to six months in most cases. Because of this, she was comfortable saying to this couple that, no, she couldn't be available next week because of her premarital counseling requirements, but that she could be available the following month.

3. Finally, what about the woman in your congregation who attends faithfully, but who wants to marry a man about whom you have serious reservations?

These are probably the hardest cases. As the woman's pastor, you may want to share your reservations. But what do you do if it becomes obvious that she is going to marry the man anyway? Should you perform the marriage or refuse, with the possibility of alienating this member? There are no easy answers, and most pastors decide these on a case-by-case basis. Pastor Winter, after meeting with the member and her fiancé, felt strongly that since this woman had a history of dating dangerous men, and since her fiancé appeared to be an alcoholic, she could perform the service only after the couple had sought professional premarital counseling for one year. Unfortunately upon hearing this, the woman became angry with Pastor Winter, left the church, and was married by a secular officiant the following week.

# Premarital Counseling

Your initial meeting with the couple serves several purposes. First, it gives you an opportunity to get to know them better and provides you with information so that you can make an informed decision about the overall style and tone of the service. Some questions that pastors like to ask during the initial meeting are:

How did the couple meet? How long have they known each other? When did they decide to get married? What are some of their common interests? How do they get along with their respective in-laws? How much thought have they given to what their life together will look like? For example, do they plan on having children? Right away? If they've already started living together, do they think marriage will change things? How?

Second, the initial meeting allows you to share any particular requirements you or the church may have: the number of premartial meetings, cleaning deposits or fees that the church imposes, regulations regarding the use of the organ, and any other matters.

Finally, at the end of the first meeting, some pastors give homework to the couple. For example, *Please Understand Me II* by David Keirsey and Marilyn Bates follows the basic Myers-Briggs psychological assessment and has a survey in the back that can be helpful for premartial counseling. The results of the survey can be used during a later meeting with the couple to illustrate the uniqueness of how people learn and share, and how important it is to respect each other's differences.

During subsequent meetings, the pastor may also want to explore specific topics with the couple, such as their motives for getting married, how they approach conflict resolution, and their attitudes toward money, sex, and each other's family and friends. (Handouts to facilitate these discussions are at the end of this chapter.)

Regardless of how many meetings you decide to have with the couple, you will need to reserve time during the final session to go over the vows with the couple and to talk with them about the service itself. Don't forget to collect the names (and accurate spelling) of everyone who is participating in the service, including the couple's parents. Then walk them through the service step-by-step.

Specific wedding liturgies vary, but most follow the same general order: gathering, acolytes, seating of parents, procession of wedding party, opening greeting, declaration of intent by the man and the woman, the father's presentation of the bride (optional), Scripture, sermon, exchange of vows, exchange of rings, declaration of the marriage, kiss (here or at end of service), blessing of marriage, thanksgiving prayers, and dismissal. Perry H. Biddle's *Abingdon Marriage Manual*, second edition, is an excellent resource for planning services. As you discuss the liturgy with the couple, have them answer the following questions:

1. Will there be bulletins? If so, will the couple or the pastor provide them?
2. Will there be a guest registry? If yes, have they arranged for a greeter to attend the registry?
3. What music will be used as guests are seated? Who will provide it?
4. Will one of the ushers act as acolyte or will another person(s) light the candles?
5. Will a special song or vocal be used before or after the parents are seated?
6. Will an aisle runner need to be rolled out after the parents are seated?
7. What processional music will be used for the wedding party?
8. What processional music will be used for the bride's entrance?

The most complicated part of the service, logistically, is the procession.

1. Which members of the party will take their positions up front prior to the beginning of the procession and the processional music?

The pastor usually takes his or her position up front prior to the beginning of the procession. He or she can formally walk in or enter through a side entrance, but however the pastor enters, it is most often done without any special music. The pastor can be accompanied by the groom, the groom and best man, or the groom with all of his groomsmen (if the groomsmen are not formally processing in with music later).

2. Will any members of the party individually process down the aisle?

If processing individually, the groomsmen may proceed down the aisle by themselves, followed by the bridesmaids, followed by the ring bearer, flower girl, and finally by the bride, herself. (Alternatively, as the bride nears the altar, the groom can advance up the aisle to meet her and then walk back with her to the front.)

3. Or will members of the party walk together in pairs down the aisle?

The bridesmaids can be escorted by the groomsmen. The ring bearer and flower girl can process in together. And the bride can be escorted by her father, or she and the groom can process in together. Traditionally, a woman is escorted on a man's right arm, which means that she will need to cross in front of the man as she arrives at her final place up front, but some choose to have the woman escorted on the man's left arm to avoid this crossover.

The wedding party's final arrangement should look like this:

| Groom's guests | Bride's guests |
|---|---|
| Note: The parents should have reserved seats up front. | |
| Groomsman #2, Groomsman #1 | Bridesmaid # 1, Bridesmaid #2 |
| Best Man | Maid of Honor |
| Ring Bearer | Flower Girl |
| | Bride's Father |
| Groom | Bride |
| Minister | |
| Front of Church | |

Additional questions include:

1. Will the father be escorting and presenting the bride?
2. Will the minister be reading the Scripture, or are there readers?
3. Does the couple have any requested Scripture readings?
4. Does the couple want to remain standing during the entire service or at certain times will they be seated, such as during the sermon?
5. Will the couple recite the traditional vows, add their own vows, read a poem, or add to the vows in any other way?
6. Will both bride and groom be receiving rings?
7. Where does the couple want to place the traditional "you may now kiss your bride"? After the declaration of the marriage or at the end of the service?
8. Will the couple be lighting a unity candle?
9. Will the couple use kneelers or receive the blessing while standing?
10. Will holy communion be celebrated at the wedding?

# The Wedding Rehearsal

The wedding rehearsal is usually held the night before the wedding and should take between half an hour and an hour. The rehearsal gives the pastor the opportunity to meet and greet everyone, and it gives each participant a chance to practice the service with musical accompaniment. Here the decisions the couple made previously can be tested and modified as needed.

Expect people to act somewhat hesitant and awkward at first; this is normal. If the couple has employed a wedding planner, he or she should be included, as he or she can be quite helpful both during the rehearsal and on the wedding day itself. That said, however, the pastor has the final say about how the service is performed, and most wedding planners are sensitive to this.

A typical wedding has three acts—the entrance, the wedding, and the dismissal. Start the rehearsal with act three. Position everyone up front where they will be at the conclusion of the service, then ask them to practice leaving (processing out of) the sanctuary. Next have them regroup and practice processing in.

Because a marriage license is required before you can legally perform the service, the rehearsal is also the time to collect the license from the couple.

On the wedding day itself, the pastor should make himself or herself available well before the service starts. Perhaps stop in and say a prayer with the bride and the groom—separately since most couples will not want to see each other until the service starts—then remind them to relax and enjoy themselves.

# Funerals

When a member of your congregation dies, you may be present at the time of death, notified shortly after the death, or not notified until the funeral director calls you. Regardless, it is important to meet with the surviving relatives as soon as possible.

Immediately following a death, a pastor's focus is solely on being a caring presence to the family, *not* planning the funeral. People react to death in a variety of ways: with silence, fear, anger, tears, uncontrolled grief, busyness, talkativeness, shock, and so on. It is crucial that you let people grieve however they grieve. Now is not the time to try to counsel them, or in your awkwardness, offer platitudes, say anything to try and fix the situation, or explain it theologically. Most pastors have found that the greatest gift they can offer is a steady, silent presence. When you do speak, focus on the accomplishments and admirable qualities of the deceased or share something personal: "I remember the first time I met Bob, I was trying to figure out how to turn on the church's furnace. He went down and showed me how, step by step. I'm going to miss that about him. He was always so helpful."

# Planning the Funeral Service

Within the first couple of days after the death, meet with the family to discuss the funeral arrangements. If the family has not yet been to the funeral home, offer to go with them, to help pick out a casket, and make the other arrangements. Either at this time, or shortly thereafter during a home visit, plan the rest of the service. Find out:

1. Will there be bulletins for the service?
2. Where will the service take place? (church, funeral home, graveside?)
3. Does the family have any particular preferences? (certain Scripture, hymns, or photographic displays?)
4. Who will participate in the service? (relatives, friends, other ministers?)
5. How will they participate? (music, Scripture, a eulogy?)
6. What remarks about the person might you include in your sermon?
7. Finally, was the person in the military or any other order (such as police), and if so, will certain rituals be performed before, during, or after the service? For example, veterans are entitled to a flag presentation at the graveside.

# Funeral Sermons

A funeral sermon serves two purposes: one, to proclaim the gospel in the face of death, and two, to sum up the life of the deceased while looking toward the future with hope. It is vital that pastors avoid romanticizing or trivializing death.

Example of romanticizing death: "God surely needed a new angel in heaven."

Example of trivializing death: "At last, she's gone home to be with God," or "She is in God's hands now."

Make sure to give thanks to God for the life of the deceased and to share something of that life. Don't be afraid to include a funny or charming story about the person, though do make sure it depicts the deceased in a positive light. For example:

Everyone who knew Sam, knew that he hated Lobell's Department Store, hated it with a passion. Not only did he refuse to shop there, but he forbade anyone in his family to shop there as well. Sam had hated Lobell's so long that he, himself, had even forgotten why. Unfortunately Sam's feelings proved difficult for Sam's wife and daughter, who loved Lobell's. But nevertheless, they tried to honor his wishes. I was with Sam the night he died, and he specifically asked me to go get his family. Unable to speak, he scribbled on a notebook in big, bold letters:

*Now you won't have to sneak around to shop at Lobell's anymore.* Then he drew a big smiley face. That was Sam; even during the worst of times, his playfulness and sense of humor couldn't help making you smile.

In addition to sharing memories about the deceased, a funeral sermon serves to remind people of God's trustworthiness. People look to the pastor to make sense of death—to the extent that death can ever make sense—and to affirm that God can be trusted both in life and in the mystery of death. As a minister of the gospel, your job, especially at times of great grief, is to represent God by speaking the good news, which is *not* that death is no big deal, but rather that God is even greater than death. Perhaps more than any other time, at the funeral people will be listening to what you say in your sermon.

# The Visitation (or Wake) and Viewing

Try to make an appearance during the public visitation to check on the family and to let them know that you care and are praying for them. If possible, also try to be with the family the next day for their final, private viewing before the casket is closed. Ideally, the casket will be closed prior to the start of the service—and it should be closed for funerals in the church—but some funeral homes prefer open caskets, in which case the final viewing will take place following the service.

The funeral director typically takes care of giving the pastor the honorarium, though sometimes the family will do this directly. Accepting money for a funeral can be awkward, especially if the deceased was a member of the church, but the honorarium can be graciously accepted and then given to the memorial fund of the deceased, if you so desire.

# Follow-up with the Family

Finally, mark your calendar so that you'll remember to check in with the surviving family two weeks, two months, and six months following the death. Perhaps schedule a visit during major holidays and on the anniversary of the death too. Grief, by definition, is a process. People may seem fine one week and then the next, fall back into depression. A good book for pastors is Elisabeth Kübler-Ross's *On Death and Dying* because it identifies the typical stages of grief: (1) denial and isolation, (2) anger, (3) bargaining, (4) depression, (5) acceptance and hope. Another suggestion, and one that can also be shared with someone who has recently suffered a loss, is Nicholas Wolterstorff's *Lament for a Son*. Wolterstorff explores the connections between the

God who suffers and the suffering of humanity; and as he finds himself grieving the loss of his son, he rediscovers the Christian blessing of hope.

This same blessing of hope is one that you, as pastor, must bring to people, whether in the joyous contexts of baptism and Christian marriage, or the mournful setting of a funeral.

# Pastor's Checklist

## Additional Resources

Perry H. Biddle. *The Abingdon Marriage Manual.* Nashville: Abingdon Press, 1994.

Michael L. Kirkindoll. *The Hospital Visit: A Pastor's Guide.* Abingdon Press, 2001.

John S. Mansell. *The Funeral: A Pastor's Guide.* Abingdon Press, 1998.

## Suggested Wedding Scriptures

Genesis 1:26-28, 31a (Creation of Man and Woman)
Song of Solomon 2:8-13; 8:6-7 (Love Is Strong as Death)
Isaiah 63:7-9 (The Steadfast Love of the Lord)
Micah 6:6-8 (What Does God Require)
Psalms 23, 33, 34, 67, 100, 112, 148, and 150

Matthew 5:1-14 (the Beatitudes)
Matthew 7:21, 24-27 (A House Built upon a Rock)
Matthew 22:35-40 (Love, the Greatest Commandment)
Mark 10:42-45 (True Greatness)
John 2:1-11 (The Marriage Feast of Cana)
John 15:9-17 (Remain in Christ's Love)

Romans 12:1-2, 9-18 (The Life of a Christian)
1 Corinthians 13 (The Greatest of These Is Love)
Philippians 4:4-9 (Rejoice in the Lord)
Colossians 3:12-17 (Live in Love and Thanksgiving)
I John 3:18-24 (Love One Another)
I John 4:7-12 (God Is Love)

## Suggested Funeral Scriptures

Isaiah 25:1, 6-9 (God Will Swallow Up Death)
Isaiah 40:1-8, 28-31 (Comfort My People)
Isaiah 43:1-7, 18-19 (God Will Deliver)
Ecclesiastes 3:1-11 (A Time for Everything)
Micah 6:6-8 (What Does God Require)
Psalms 23, 27, 42, 46, 84, 91, 121, and 130

Matthew 5:1-12 (Beatitudes)
Matthew 11:25-30 (Come to Me All Who Labor)
Matthew 28:1-10 (Jesus' Resurrection)
Luke 12:22-34 (Do Not Be Anxious)
John 3:13-17 (Eternal Life)
John 14:1-7, 18-21, 25-27 (Jesus' Farewell Discourse)
John 16:12-24 (Sorrow Will Become Joy)
John 20:1-10 and 20:11-18 and/or 20:19-23 (Resurrection)

Romans 6:3-11 (Dying and Rising with Christ)
Romans 8:18-30 (Future Glory)
Romans 14:7-9 (Christ, Lord of Dead and Living)
1 Corinthians 15:1-8, 12-20, 35-44 (The Nature of the Resurrection)
2 Corinthians 4:5-18 (Glory in God)
Ephesians 1:3-14 (Spiritual Blessings in Christ)
1 Thessalonians 4:13–5:11 (The Coming of God)
2 Timothy 4:6-8, 17-18 (I've Fought the Good Fight)
Revelation 21:1-7, 22:1-5 (The New Jerusalem)

# MOTIVES FOR GETTING MARRIED

## (Premarital Counseling Handout)

Unhelpful Motives

1. You marry because you don't know who you are without the other person.
2. You marry in order to escape loneliness or feel better about yourself.
3. You marry to get away from a bad situation: home, dead end job, and so on.
4. You are afraid of being alone in the world and want security at any price.
5. You marry because others expect you to, not because you really want to.
6. You want to feel important, and so you "rescue" someone who needs you.
7. You mistake strong physical attraction or infatuation for love.

Helpful Motives

1. You have a good self-esteem and sense of personal identity, and you wish to continue to grow as a person in the context of a committed relationship.
2. You are happy, have a full life with interests, friends, values, and hopes, and you want to share this life with another person, even as he or she shares his or her life with you.
3. You are not running away from something, but instead are looking forward to building an environment of security, esteem, affection, compassion, and honesty with your spouse in a healthy marriage where you feel safe and can raise children, should you decide to have children.
4. You have found someone who enables you to become a better person and who supports you in your life's ambitions: someone who is honest and encouraging, rejoices at your successes, and commiserates with you when things do not work out.
5. You truly want a marriage with this person, even knowing that all marriages come with moments of frustration, conflict, hurt, and disappointment.

Reproduced from *Ready, Set, Lead: The New Pastor's Guide to Starting Ministry* by Lynda C. Ward and Steven P. Brey. Copyright © 2006 by Abingdon Press. Reproduced by permission.

6. You want a relationship grounded in mutuality and respect: one where you make healthy sacrifices for the other person, but where they also make sacrifices for you.
7. You have found someone with whom to share your sexuality, not just as a pleasurable end in itself, but as a way of growing in emotional intimacy with your partner.

# Conflict Resolution

## (Premarital Counseling Handout)

Building Mutual Respect

1. Do you each go to the other for advice, or does one person solely rely upon the other?
2. Do you both compromise on occasion, or does one of you feel that he or she is always "giving in"?
3. Can you talk through your differences calmly, or do discussions frequently result in arguments? Can you each give a current example of a topic on which you disagree?
4. Do you both feel that you have a "voice" when it comes to making important decisions? Are you willing to take each other's point of view into account before making a final decision? Can you give an example?

The Dos of Fighting Fairly

- Do pick an appropriate time to discuss controversial topics, and check with your partner to make sure that it is a good time.
- Do be willing to compromise: Remember, neither of you is likely to be 100 percent correct in an argument, and there are no winners and losers when friends fight—in the end you either both win or you both lose.
- Do keep the discussion specific to the issue at hand.
- Do keep things in perspective: if your spouse is typically a compassionate person, keep this in mind as you discuss the insensitive or hurtful thing that he or she just did.
- Do pay attention to your body language: maintain eye contact, keep your voice calm, arms uncrossed, and avoid threatening postures or gestures.
- Do listen to what the other person is saying and honestly try to hear the other person's point of view *before* responding and sharing your own view. (Make a habit of waiting at least three seconds after your spouse stops talking before you respond. Acknowledge and validate your spouse's feelings by rephrasing your spouse's statements to make sure that you have understood correctly.)

Reproduced from *Ready, Set, Lead: The New Pastor's Guide to Starting Ministry* by Lynda C. Ward and Steven P. Brey. Copyright © 2006 by Abingdon Press. Reproduced by permission.

- Do point out areas where your spouse is doing well, as opposed to simply criticizing his or her weaknesses.
- Do make the effort, even during a fight, to be vulnerable and say "I was wrong" or "I'm sorry."

The Don'ts of Fighting Fairly

- Don't try to discuss any issue while your spouse is venting anger. Acknowledge the other person's anger, then wait until he or she calms down before initiating a discussion.
- Don't argue in front of an audience, friends or relatives.
- Don't ignore or walk away from a conflict, though strategic time-outs can be useful to allow each other time to cool off.
- Don't make the argument personal by attacking your spouse's character or personality. For example, say, "I wish you would put the dishes away when you are done," not "You are such a slob."
- Don't accuse or use "you" statements. Instead, try to share your thoughts in terms of "I feel. . . ." For example, "I felt hurt when you forgot to call me this afternoon," as opposed to "You never call me anymore. I guess you just don't care."
- Don't bring up old issues to support or justify your behavior or to critique theirs. For example, don't say, "You did this same thing last month!"
- Don't use words that exaggerate, such as "always" and "never."
- Don't make threats or give ultimatums, and never, under any circumstances, hit or throw something at the other person.

# DISCUSSION QUESTIONS FOR PREMARITAL COUNSELING

Money

(*Note: The couple should prepare a sample budget and bring it with them prior to discussing these questions.*)

1. Who prepared the budget that you brought to this meeting?
2. Do you have similar spending habits, or if not, how do they differ? Can each of you list your priorities in terms of spending and saving?
3. Have you worked out a way of handling the finances that is agreeable to both of you, e.g., who will be the primary wage earner, who will pay the bills, how much discretionary money will each of you have to spend?
4. What is your ideal income? For example, would you both be comfortable living a middle-class lifestyle, or does one of you want to afford a six-bedroom mansion?
5. Are you comfortable being honest with each other about your spending habits and income, or would you prefer to hide some of your money or purchases from the other?

Sex

1. Are you comfortable talking with each other about sex?
2. Have you openly discussed birth control options and past sexual history, including frank discussions about sexually transmitted diseases?
3. Is your sexual relationship leading you to greater emotional intimacy, or is it being used to conceal problems in the relationship?
4. How important would you each say that sex is in this relationship on a scale of 1 to 10 (10 being the most important thing in the relationship).

Family and Friends

1. How would each of you describe your relationship with your future in-laws? Have you talked about the role that your in-laws will play?

2. Have you discussed how many children you want, and what you will do if things do not work out as planned?
3. Have you talked about how you will raise your children, including issues of discipline and the role that religious beliefs will play?
4. How do you feel about each other's friends? What role will friends play in your married life? Do you think it is possible to keep your current friendships with friends who are single after you are married, or do you believe that now that you are a couple, your primary friends should be couples as well?

# THE WEDDING PARTY WORKSHEET

Bride:                              Groom:

Flower Girl:                        Ring Bearer:

Maid/Matron of Honor:              Best Man:

Bridesmaid:                        Groomsman/Usher:

Bridesmaid:                        Groomsman/Usher:

Bridesmaid:                        Groomsman/Usher:

Bridesmaid:                        Groomsman/Usher:

Bridesmaid:                        Groomsman/Usher:


Bride's Mother:                    Groom's Mother:

Bride's Father:                    Groom's Father:

Other Bride's Family:              Other Groom's Family:


Greeter/Guest Book Attendant:

Acolytes:

Special Music:

Reader(s):

# FUNERAL PLANNING WORKSHEET

Name _____ Date of Death _____ Age _____
Visitation: Place _____ Date _____ Time _____
Funeral: Place _____ Date _____ Time _____
Place of Final Interment _____

Coffin open or closed before service?　　　　During service?
Committal service at graveside?
Church luncheon to follow?

*Participants from church:*
Pastor(s) _____
Pianist/Organist _____
Ushers _____
Other _____

*Participation from friends/family:*
Special music _____
Readers _____
Eulogy speakers _____
Pallbearers _____
_____
_____

*Scripture:*
First Reading _____
Psalm or Response _____
Second Reading _____
Gospel Reading _____

*Music:*
First _____
Second _____
Third _____
Other _____

Reproduced from *Ready, Set, Lead: The New Pastor's Guide to Starting Ministry* by Lynda C. Ward and Steven P. Brey. Copyright © 2006 by Abingdon Press. Reproduced by permission.

Other rites or special arrangements: _____

Survivors:_____

_____

Notes for follow-up: _____

_____
_____
_____
_____
_____
_____
_____
_____
_____
_____
_____
_____
_____
_____
_____
_____
_____
_____

# CHAPTER FIVE

# PREPARE FOR VISITATION, COUNSELING, AND CRISIS MINISTRY

Nothing is more vital to ministry than for a pastor to develop and maintain relationships and to act as a companion, mentor, counselor, and spiritual guide. Relationships are best built through visitations and counseling, but many ministers feel awkward and unsure of what to say or do. The goal of this chapter is to point you to skills that will help you become better acquainted with your role as spiritual companion, guide, and counselor.

## Essential Conversational Skills

Whether during home visits, formal counseling, or talking with a visitor at your church, your primary goal is to do more than talk: it is to build relationships. Not all of your relationships will be the same, however; for example, acting as a counselor to a young man who is struggling with his faith is very different from visiting a homebound member who depends on you for companionship. But no matter the situation, there are some essential skills and rules for conversation that apply.

## Look Forward to the Visit or Appointment

The right attitude makes all the difference. A pastor who looks forward to a conversation is more likely to be open and relaxed. Remember, each encounter is an opportunity for ministry. Welcome the opportunity to help your members discover the presence of God in their lives.

## Prepare

Always review your notes from a previous session if counseling, or if visiting, your visitation record. Take a minute to recall the purpose of the visit or meeting and jot down a few questions you may want to ask. Then consider the person with whom you are meeting: What do you know about them? What are their interests, hopes, dreams, fears? What is going on in their life? Or if you do not know them, what would you like to know? Spend time praying for each person prior to meeting with them.

## Be Interested

You've probably heard the saying, "Everybody has a story." Everybody *does* have a unique history, hobby, job, or lifelong dream that has shaped or influenced him or her in a particular way. Be interested in each member's story. Remember, every conversation reveals something about its participants.

## Practice Active Listening Skills

A good habit is to repeat what someone just said in the form of a question or statement (or a combination of the two). This not only helps clarify, it also demonstrates that you are listening. For example, if a member says, "Pastor, I left several messages. I can't stop worrying about my test results," try this response: "I understand that you are worried. You left several messages at your doctor's office?"

## Ask Leading Questions

Avoid questions that have one-word or short answers such as no, yes, fine, good, or, I don't know. Instead, ask leading questions. For example, replace "How are you doing?" with "What are you thankful for today?" Or instead of saying,

"Are you enjoying the warm weather?" try, "When the weather is warm, I spend more time in my garden. How are you spending these warm spring days?"

## Monitor Yourself

In any conversation, pay attention to the tone and volume of your voice, your body language, how much or little you are talking, whether or not you are making eye contact, and your energy level. Consciously check to make sure your actions and body language are appropriate to the situation and adjust accordingly. For instance, if the person with whom you are talking is shy, you may find yourself talking too much to fill the awkward silences, or if someone is angry, you might speak too loudly. But regardless of the situation, your goal remains the same: to provide a safe and comfortable environment where people can be vulnerable and share their true needs and concerns. Monitor yourself to make sure you are facilitating the conversation and not blocking it. With shy people, relax and be patient with awkward silences; perhaps make a single point, "Everyone is talking about that play we had at the church last week," then ask a leading question, "I was glad you attended, what did you think?" Then wait for their response.

## Set Appropriate Time Limits

In terms of counseling, set a policy, and let people know it ahead of time. For example, say, "My counseling sessions are one hour. Can I schedule you from 2:00 to 3:00 P.M.?" Or for visits, set a personal time limit and try to leave within ten minutes of the time you set. Between fifteen and thirty minutes is best for in-home visits, unless you have been invited to lunch, dinner, or a party. Try to limit hospital visits to fifteen minutes.

## Plan an Exit Strategy

Every pastor encounters people with whom it is difficult to end a conversation, so have a few exit strategies prepared to use in these situations. In terms of counseling, frequently a person will bring up an important issue late in the session. Because counseling is a more structured conversation, it will be easier to say, "Let me remind you that we only have ten minutes left, so we'll need to put that topic on our agenda for next time." Visits, however, can be more difficult. Some pastors like to use certain words or phrases at the beginning of the visit to hint at its length: "I'm glad you had a few minutes to visit with me this morning," or "I'm between appointments, but I wanted to stop by," or "I'm just popping in for a quick visit to see how you are doing today." But there will still be times when a direct exit strategy is needed. Choose strategies that best fit your style and comfort level. To end a visit, some pastors stand and ask if they can use the restroom or get a glass of water, then afterwards say, "I really must be going." Other pastors politely interrupt and say that they are sorry, but they have an appointment or somewhere else that they need to be. Another strategy is to let the person make a final point, then offer a conclusion: "This has been a good visit, why don't we end our time together with a short prayer."

# Visitation

The purpose of a visit is to check in periodically with members and do a quick assessment of their needs, as well as to offer a physical reminder that the church cares for its members. The focus of a visit is the member who is being visited: whatever thoughts, feelings, joys, or concerns she or he has on that day. Should a personal issue arise during the visit that needs more time than this visit allows, schedule a follow-up visit or an appointment at your office.

In terms of calling prior to a visit, many pastors find it difficult to decide if they should call first or stop by unannounced. For a new pastor, it is best to call at least thirty minutes prior to the visit to ask if it is all right to visit. Then over time, as relationships are established, you can note the people who prefer phone calls first and those who welcome unannounced visits.

Some members prefer not to be visited in their homes. An easy way to determine your members' preferences is to have a sign-up sheet available during Sunday worship. Ask members (and visitors too, when appropriate) to sign and indicate the times that are best for visits. Divide the sheet into columns such as, "Morning," "Afternoon," "Evening," "Anytime," and "I prefer a phone call instead of a visit." Sometimes a person who prefers not to be visited in their home will accept an invitation to meet somewhere for coffee. Ask this when you call them. But always visit members who are homebound or in nursing homes, and try to check in regularly with those who are sick, recently bereaved, or anyone who seems particularly stressed or appears depressed. Finally, don't neglect youth and children. Be sure to touch base with them while visiting the homes of their parents, and especially for teens, look for creative ways to check in with them. Some pastors like to invite several youth at a time to a restaurant for dinner; this gives them the freedom to talk without their parents present.

# Visiting the Sick

For hospital, hospice, or nursing home visits, it is acceptable to stop by unannounced, but call and ask for scheduled visitation hours first. Sometimes clergy are not bound by posted hours, but unless there is an emergency or special need, try to stop by during the regular hours. When you arrive, if the patient is out of the room, undergoing an examination or tests, or is asleep, check at a nurse's station to see if it would be best to wait or if it is all right to wake the person; if not, leave a calling card with a brief note to let the person know that you stopped by.

During a hospital visit it is fine to:

- Touch the patient (but make sure you've washed your hands first)
- Ask if there is anything you can do for the patient (such as get a magazine, turn off the television, pour a glass of water)
- Ask about the patient's health (but don't get too personal)
- Encourage the person to talk about his or her health or situation (be sure to sympathize, but don't indulge self-pity, as this may be more harmful than helpful)
- Directly ask about the patient's spiritual health; be open to discussing faith issues
- Be cheerful and positive (but don't talk too much)
- Bring the person a recent church newsletter, inspirational book, pamphlet, or other religious material
- Read Scripture and pray with the person

Should a patient bring up an important issue just as you are ready to leave, it is all right to lengthen the visit by five or ten minutes, but always make sure that the patient's energy is not overtaxed. If the patient is undergoing surgery, is dying, or has a special need, the visit may need to be extended by minutes or even hours.

# Counseling

In terms of confidentiality, take care not to repeat things that you learn in private about a parishioner, unless you are certain that the parishioner does not mind. For example, a member asks for prayers because she is scheduled for some medical tests next week; don't assume that she therefore wants the entire congregation to know. Get her permission first. Also parishioners will come to you to discuss personal matters, such as problems in their marriage or feelings of guilt over something they have done. Always be aware of your professional and legal obligation to keep such conversations confidential. The only exceptions to this rule are when physical harm might come to someone because of your silence, when you are required by law to break confidence, such as when child abuse is suspected, or when it is necessary to consult with other professionals, though in this last case the person's name can be changed.

It is best when counseling a person of the opposite sex to avoid even the appearance of impropriety by only offering counseling in your office at church or in some other public place. And without breaking confidentiality by naming the person or revealing specific details, someone else—your spouse, your ecclesiastical superiors, a trusted colleague—should be aware that you are engaged in counseling. In fact personal supervision is almost always recommended when you are engaged in formal counseling.

Another important rule to remember when counseling anyone is: When in doubt, refer to a mental health professional. Wise pastors will do their homework and make a list of credible, professional counselors or psychiatrists, to whom they feel comfortable referring members. Talk with health care professionals, funeral directors, colleagues, advocacy and crisis centers, and police officers in your area and ask for recommendations. Then call, introduce yourself, ask about specialties, typical rates, and if referrals are accepted.

Never attempt to counsel a person for any issue for which you have not been specifically trained. Typically, pastors are not trained to deal with severe depression or anxiety, alcoholism or other addictions, situations of abuse, or personality disorders such as histrionic, antisocial, or oppositional-defiant disorders. While there is usually a spiritual component to a majority of these, a pastor must never take sole responsibility for counseling in these situations. In conjunction with a psychiatrist or counselor, a pastor can offer ongoing spiritual support and guidance to members who are in professional counseling, and many mental health professionals are eager to work with pastors who provide spiritual care, but church members will first need to give their written permission, so that you and the counselor can communicate with each other.

Pastors *can* provide counseling for any issue for which they have been specifically trained (some pastors are certified spiritual guides, others are licensed social workers or pastoral counselors), for short-term topics dealing with matters of faith, and for transitional issues: preparing for baptism or marriage, grieving the loss of a loved one, healing from an injury or dealing with an illness, the transition after a divorce, when children leave home, when someone must move to a nursing home or assisted living facility, or other life transitions, all of which involve some degree of mild, situational depression or anxiety where a pastor's support and wisdom can be beneficial. While many couples approach ministers for marriage counseling, it is best to refer these couples to professional counseling unless it is an issue that can be resolved in no more than four meetings and with both partners present.

Pastors should never undertake long-term or ongoing counseling of any kind. A good rule for pastors is that no matter what the issue, if it cannot be resolved in four meetings (one month), it is best to refer to a professional, but to still be available for ongoing support or supplemental spiritual guidance.

# Crisis Ministry

At some point, every minister will be called during a time of crisis. This can be any crisis: a youth calls because she crashed her parent's new car into a tree, or a gunman has opened fire at a factory where many of your members are employed. What follows is a case study and example of how to handle a crisis.

Pastor Pruett answered his phone at 4:00 A.M. on Saturday. It was Luke Robbins, a widowed single father who lived alone about three miles away. His only child, Stephanie, was at college. Luke sounded as if he was having trouble catching his breath: "Pastor, this is Luke, I'm sorry to wake you. It's Stephanie, my daughter. Someone called and said something about a party at her sorority house and a fire. The alarms and sprinklers didn't go off. The house caught fire. I don't know what to do. She's over a thousand miles away."

Pastor Pruett replied, "Luke, I'm glad you called. Did they give you any specific information about Stephanie?"

"No. The person who called, I didn't write down her name, I can't remember. She said she would call back as soon as she knew anything about Steph. She said she was calling all the parents. Some girls had been taken to the hospital, but she didn't have names."

Pastor Pruett balanced the phone on his shoulder and pulled on his clothes. "Luke, I'm getting dressed now. I'll be right over. While you wait for me, see if you can find a list of the names and numbers for the sorority, or any other contact numbers. Turn on the television to a national news channel. I'll grab my coat and be right over. Watch for my car."

## *Plan Ahead for Times of Crisis*

Before someone in crisis calls you, it is good to have a crisis plan:

1. Name the crisis. Find out what the crisis is, with as many details as you can obtain.
2. Who does the crisis involve? If more than one person, make a list of all parties.
3. Who needs or requires immediate contact?

4. Take action to contact the appropriate people.
5. Ask yourself: Where am I needed most?

# Control Emotions

During a crisis it is important to monitor your own emotions. You will need to be the voice of reason, so remain calm, and even if you are alarmed, frightened, or otherwise emotional, try to control those emotions until after you have dealt with the crisis. But be sure to let others express their emotions without asking them to calm down, unless their emotions are preventing you from dealing with the crisis.

One way to help people manage their emotions during the crisis is to give them a task, something that they can easily do. In our example, note that Pastor Pruett tells Luke Robbins (1) to look for a list, (2) to turn on the television, and (3) to watch for the car.

# Stick with the Facts

It is vital that you deal only with facts. Never guess or make assumptions. Even if it appears to you that no one survived a crash, do not assume that anyone is injured or dead until this has been confirmed by an official person with access to accurate information. Also avoid making decisions for people. With facts in hand, do present the appropriate information to all of the parties involved, then help them consider their options. Let's return to our example:

> When Pastor Pruett arrived at Luke's house, Luke had the television on a twenty-four-hour news channel, had tried to call back the person who had called him (the line was busy), and had located last year's sorority roster with the home addresses and phone numbers of all the girls in the sorority. Luke had also started packing.
>
> Pastor Pruett looked over the sorority list and saw that there were two names of alumni sponsors and at least one parent who lived in the city where the school was located. He underlined them. Next, he got on his cell phone, called information, and got the phone number for one of the hospitals in the area and for the city's police. He called the police first. He introduced himself, explained the dilemma, and asked: Do you have any reports of a fire at a sorority house? Is someone with up-to-date information about the fire available to speak with me directly? To what hospital were the injured taken? What other information do you have at this time?

From the police, Pastor Pruett was able to confirm that there was a fire at the sorority house following a party. He was also told that the fire department was still on the scene, that there were both injuries and fatalities, and that the injured were either being taken to Southside Hospital or Palm Valley Hospital, which had a burn center. He was given the number for both.

"I got in touch with the police," Pastor Pruett said to Luke, "and I was able to confirm that there was a fire, that the fire department is on the scene, and that they are taking the injured to either Southside or Palm Valley hospital, but there is no specific information at this time about who was injured." Then he added, "Luke, if you want to take the next flight out, I can stay here and answer your phone. I'll use my cell phone to call the hospitals and keep you up-to-date on what I learn. Or if you want to wait until you get more specific information before making any travel plans, I can stay and wait with you."

Luke thought for a moment, then said, "Can I use your phone to call the airport?"

Luke learned that the next flight left at 6:30 A.M. It was almost 5:00 A.M. now, so he booked a seat. He then grabbed his own cell phone, gave Pastor Pruett the number, and left for the airport.

Around 7:30 A.M., the phone rang at the Robbin's house. Pastor Pruett answered and found a tearful Stephanie on the line. She was at the hospital with some burns on her arms and hands, but her roommate had died. Pastor Pruett got the name of the hospital and a number where she could be reached, then told her that her dad was already on a plane headed her way.

Remember, the best time to discuss issues of faith with people in crisis is after the crisis is under control or is over. While it would have been appropriate for Pastor Pruett to say a prayer for Stephanie with Luke at the house before he left for the airport, it would not have been appropriate to engage him in a discussion about his feelings or faith at that time. But if the crisis involves an injury that needs surgery, an extended waiting period, or someone who is dying, it may be appropriate to pray and discuss issues of faith.

During extended visits with people, such as at the hospital when a loved one is undergoing surgery, pay attention to the whole person: spirit, mind, and body. Say a prayer with them and address their spiritual needs, but see if there are other ways to serve them too. Sometimes they may want to talk about a faith matter, but they might just want to chat and distract themselves from the anxiety and boredom of sitting in a hospital waiting room. Consider also their physical needs: offer to get them food, something to read, or volunteer to wait in the room while they walk to stretch their legs. Remember, in a time of crisis, sometimes simply being helpful is the best ministry.

# Pastor's Checklist

Beverly, Urias. *The Places You Go: Caring for Your Congregation Monday Through Saturday*. Abingdon Press, 2003.

Biddle, Perry H., Jr. *Abingdon Hospital Visitation Manual*. Abingdon Press, 1988.
   This book includes information about special visits, such as visiting the dying or visiting patients with cancer or AIDS.

Capps, Donald. *Life Cycle Theory and Pastoral Care*. Fortress Press, 1983.
   Capps builds upon psychologist Erik Erikson's work and discusses how people deal with different underlying, fundamental "faith issues" at different points in their lives. Understanding these basic psychological stages will help a pastor realize, for example, why most teenagers struggle with who they are, whereas young adults are often preoccupied with whom they are going to spend their lives, older adults tend to reflect back on their lives and seek value.

Clinebell, Howard. *Basic Types of Pastoral Care and Counseling*. Abingdon Press, 1984.
   In this essential pastoral care reference, Clinebell addresses such topics as crisis care, bereavement counseling, marriage enrichment, referral counseling, and how to train the laity to support pastoral care ministries.

Dann, Bucky. *Addiction: Pastoral Responses*. Abingdon Press, 2002.

Fowler, James W. *Stages of Faith*. HarperSanFrancisco, 1981.
   Fowler discusses how people's faith and their conception of God changes over their lifetime, often going through predictable stages.

Hedges-Goettl, Len. *Sexual Abuse: Pastoral Responses*. Abingdon Press, 2004.

King, Larry. *How to Talk to Anyone, Anytime, Anywhere*. New York. Crown Publishers, 1994.
   Larry King's book is great if you are shy about talking with strangers.

Weaver, Andrew, Laura Flannelly, and John D. Preston. *Counseling Survivors of Traumatic Events: A Handbook for Pastors and Other Helping Professionals*. Abingdon Press, 2003.
   A helpful Web site is http://similarminds.com. It has many of the personality tests that psychologists, therapists, and counselors use as assessment tools: Myers-Briggs, Enneagram Tests, and various personality disorder tests. Tests are offered on the Web site and are free. The results come back within seconds.

# CHAPTER SIX

# FOSTER GOOD COMMUNICATION AND MANAGE CONFLICT

How do you feel when you hear the word *conflict*? No one likes to deal with conflict, but every church, no matter how healthy, will at some point have conflict because churches are made up of people who have different ways of seeing the world. A wise pastor stays prepared for conflict so that when it happens it can be dealt with effectively and faithfully.

The best way to prepare for conflict is to practice and promote good communication in your parish. A parish that communicates well deals with conflict more productively and is more likely to overcome the stress and negative emotions that often accompany conflict. Foster good communication in your parish: practice good communications skills yourself, hold listening sessions, form a pastoral advisory committee, keep your congregation informed, give them positive feedback, share your expectations, offer guidelines, and set appropriate boundaries. Let's take a closer look at each one.

## Practice Good Communication Skills

As the church's leader, your communication style serves as a model. If you are open, honest, willing to listen, accepting of feedback, respectful of boundaries, and not afraid to admit when you have made a mistake or don't know the answer to a question, then your parishioners will be more likely to do this too. Also, be conscious of body language. Body language can influence how people perceive you and how comfortable they are in approaching and talking with you. Never underestimate the power of a smile, a firm handshake, the willingness to look people directly in the eye, a nod when you agree with someone, or the ability to laugh at yourself when necessary and to laugh with others when appropriate. If you can put people at ease with your words, actions, and attitude, you can, even in the most difficult of situations, gain their confidence and trust as a pastor.

# Hold Listening Sessions

Some pastors find it helpful to hold *listening sessions*, where no more than seven members of the congregation are invited to meet with the pastor over coffee or dessert. Typically, these members are not the church's leaders, committee heads, or guardians, but members who might not otherwise have a voice. Unlike problem-solving sessions where solutions are sought for problems and plans are made, a pastor's listening sessions are just that: an opportunity for the pastor to ask some questions and to listen while members share their hopes, dreams, and concerns for the church. Additionally, if you have senior high school students, college students, or young adults in your congregation, you may want to hold age-specific listening sessions as well. Meetings over hot dogs or pizza are a great way for the pastor to learn the interests and concerns of teens and young adults.

# Form a Pastoral Advisory Committee

A pastoral advisory committee is organized by the pastor and is made up of no more than eight mature, responsible, and faithful members who are willing to support you in your ministry. The group's purpose is to provide the space for you to problem solve or brainstorm together about possible ideas for the church. A pastoral advisory committee can be especially helpful if your church is undergoing any kind of change or growth, because this committee can give you valuable feedback and keep you informed of any miscommunication or conflict in the church. Some ministers like to rotate members of this committee, giving each of the church's trusted leaders and members a chance to serve. Rotating committee members also gives you an opportunity to hear differing opinions.

# Give Updates and Feedback

So much of what a pastor does is behind the scenes and not seen by the congregation. It is a good idea to make sure your congregation knows that you are actively caring for them, even when you are not as visible as you are on Sunday mornings. Here are some ways you can keep your church informed:

1. Give a brief update during the announcement time on Sunday, but keep it general (respecting confidentiality rules) and upbeat, for example: "I enjoyed visiting with some of our homebound members this week. Mr. Morris, who is in his nineties and still growing beautiful African violets on his window sill, sends his love to everyone," or "I spent some time organizing our membership files this week. We have been blessed to have had ten new members join us within the past two years." At times you may want to give more specific information, for example: "I donated the $100 in the pastor's discretionary fund this past week to that young couple in our community who lost everything in a fire. Let's keep them in our prayers," or "I'd like to pass along something interesting that I learned last week at the Small Church Conference." Brief updates are a casual but effective way to let members know what you do in addition to the Sunday worship service.

2. Invite suggestions. Consider placing a suggestion box in the narthex or in Sunday school rooms and mention that you check the boxes regularly. Pastors also find it helpful to say that while all suggestions are welcome, any inappropriately harsh comments that are unsigned will be filed in the trash can.

3. Publish your office hours and e-mail address in the newsletter and the bulletin. Don't forget to mention that people need not have an issue to discuss or problem to solve in order to contact you. Let them know that you welcome anyone for any reason, even if it is just for a friendly chat.

4. Make sure everyone knows that you would like to be called during times of crisis. So many times people incorrectly assume that the pastor just "knows." Be sure to ask members to keep you informed of people who are sick, or who are in the hospital, or if they know of someone who might benefit from a visit. Also look for opportunities to let your members know that you care about them even if they haven't contacted you with a need.

5. Recognize the accomplishments of others, keep the congregation informed of the efforts of the church's leaders, and be supportive of church members attending training events and seminars. Praise your congregation as much as you can for its positive and faithful actions, however small, and be sure to applaud members for their accomplishments, including youth and children.

# Share Your Expectations

If you have certain expectations, it is especially important to share them with your church's leaders and staff within your first month. For example, if your church has a history of members showing up late for meetings, and you prefer that meetings start on time, tell them that you try to be sensitive to people's busy schedules, and so you would like to start all meetings on time. To illustrate, show up early for every meeting and be in the room, prepared, and ready to start when everyone else arrives.

# Offer Guidelines

Guidelines can be beneficial when formal communication is necessary, such as at church committee meetings. An army officer named Henry Robert was once asked to preside over a church meeting and quickly found himself in a situation of chaos. Consequently, he wrote a set of rules especially for church meetings based upon parliamentary law. Some pastors like to use "Robert's Rules of Order" because they have found that by following these rules, meetings are much more productive. The rules serve to keep people on topic because everyone knows what is expected, and they give everyone a chance to speak. Robert's Rules can be purchased at any bookstore or ordered online. Based upon "Robert's Rules," the following guidelines can help church meetings run smoothly:

1. The committee chair has the official "call to order."
2. The minutes of the previous meeting are read or summarized, and corrected as necessary.
3. Each participant is given a printed copy of the meeting's agenda with topics arranged in terms of priority and with a suggested amount of time for each topic.
4. If people drift off topic, politely interrupt them, summarize the new topic, write it down, then suggest it be added to the agenda of a future meeting or discussed at another time.
5. Remind people to raise their hands if they wish to speak. This helps keep members from interrupting each another.
6. Conclude each agenda item by asking for a formal motion, if specific action is to be taken. The motion should be clearly stated, seconded, and then voted on with the results recorded in the minutes.

# Set Appropriate Boundaries

The way a parish communicates reveals something about its culture. An unhealthy church will typically use gossip, backbiting, insinuations, dishonesty, and rumors as its primary forms of communication. As a new pastor, you will find it difficult to change a community's communication style quickly, but you can establish rules and boundaries to encourage positive, respectful, and faithful communication.

While it is not necessary to make a formal announcement about your rules regarding such things as gossip, it is important that you let people know what is appropriate and what is inappropriate. For example, many pastors have found it helpful to mention in their day-to-day communication with members that they will not be acknowledging, responding to, assigning credibility to, or holding in confidence any:

1. Unsigned written communication or any information passed along without a specific name attached. For example, "I heard through the grapevine that there are some people who don't like the changes that you've made in the worship service."

   Pastor's response: "I've never trusted information that comes from the grapevine. I do appreciate your concern, and I do care about this church. But unless you can give me the names of people who don't like the changes so that I can talk with them, or you can gather these folks together so I can listen to their concerns, then I can't really respond."

2. Information that does not follow the proper rules of confidentiality. Confidentiality typically applies only in instances where it is clear that the pastor is acting as a spiritual advisor or counselor to a person, and both the pastor and the person have agreed that their relationship is one of formal counseling or spiritual guidance. Confidentiality rules can sometimes apply to pastoral visitations too. Confidentiality rules do not apply, for example, to someone stopping you in the parking lot after the service to say, "Pastor, I wanted to let you know that Jim has been spreading rumors about Susan. But I am asking you to keep this confidential, just between you and me, otherwise Jim will know that I told you."

   Pastor's response: "Bob, I appreciate your frankness. Susan has been hurt by the rumors, and of course I care about Jim too. But it is not the proper use of confidentiality to ask me not to say or do anything about this. Confidentiality is for situations of pastoral counseling or spiritual guidance. This conversation doesn't fit into either one of those categories. And confidentiality is never used to protect someone who is hurting someone else. If Jim is spreading rumors about Susan, then someone will need to talk to Jim. But I do understand your concern about Jim finding out that you told me. How about we get together and talk about this more before I say or do anything. Is there a time we can meet this evening?"

3. Unverifiable statements or statements of opinion that are not supported by facts. For example, Mary sets up an appointment and says, "Pastor, I think it was Helen who stole the money from the church bazaar cash box."

Pastor's response: "This is a serious matter, Mary. What facts do you have that led you to believe it was Helen?"

# Who Holds the Power in Your Church?

When some pastors hear the word *power* they cringe. But a church is a community; and power, for good or ill, plays an important role in all communities. However, power does not need to be a negative term. A church without faithful leaders, longtime, committed members, or active groups, all of whom hold a type of power, will never accomplish anything.

Mistakenly, some pastors assume that since *they* are the church's leader, that *they* hold the most power, but nothing could be further from the truth. A pastor does have some power, for he or she is charged with overseeing the worship services, administering the sacraments, and the ordering of the community. But the pastor's power as a leader is mostly determined by the community. A community can embrace a pastor and give that pastor a great deal of power, or it can treat the pastor as nothing more than a powerless figurehead, or it can be somewhere in between.

A prudent pastor will find out what the church's attitude is toward its pastor and seek to discover who holds the power in the church. Once you've discovered which members hold power, look more closely at their relationships with one another, with how they treat the pastor, and how they relate to the other members. The powerful people not only shape the church as a whole, they set its priorities and can determine its faithfulness. To discover who holds the power, ask yourself:

1. Who are the church's guardians (matriarchs and patriarchs)?
2. Who are the leaders (official or unofficial)?
3. What is the typical age of the leaders and guardians?
4. What is the relationship between the guardians and leaders? Are they the same people?
5. How long have leaders held their current positions?

6. What is the relationship of wealth to power?
7. How easy is it for new members to join established groups?
8. What is the personality of the church's guardians and leaders? Are they open-minded and positive? Energetic and hospitable? Compassionate and hopeful? Committed to living their faith?
9. Who in this church is typically supportive of the pastor? Is it the guardians? The church's leaders? Or new members, young adults, and youth?

In a healthy church, the relationship between the pastor, the leaders, and the guardians is a positive one, providing the structure whereby the pastor articulates the church's vision, the leaders and members work to implement this vision, and the guardians support the vision and offer their guidance and wisdom. But too often, new pastors, excited about starting a new program or trying something that they learned in their studies, fail to take into account the dynamics of power in the parish, and by doing so, they bypass the leaders and guardians. And pastors who do this suddenly find themselves without any support. This is why a pastor needs to know and understand the customs, habits, and culture of a church community before making any significant changes or starting any new programs—if a new program or change has the support of the majority of the guardians, it is likely to succeed. But if it does not have their support, it is certain to fail.

# Find the Best Solution to Conflicts

Even if you have encouraged good communication and your church is healthy, conflict will still happen. Conflict can be as minor as two people disagreeing on where to hang a poster or as serious as threats or acts of violence. No matter what the conflict, don't run from it, ignore it, or try to wish it or pray it away (though prayer can certainly help you deal with conflict). Instead, remain calm, seek to discern what solution is in the best interest of your church, then work with the members to bring about that solution.

There are three main types of conflict: conflict between a member (or members) and the pastor, conflict between the members of the community themselves, and systemic conflict, or conflict that is embedded in the community as a whole (systemic conflict typically has a history that accompanies it). The first two types of conflict can range from minor conflicts, which can be easily negotiated, to major conflicts where the pastor may need to seek help from outside the community. Systemic conflict is almost always the most serious, but that doesn't mean there isn't a solution. Let's take a look at some specific examples and consider possible solutions.

# Example of Conflict Between the Pastor and Parishioners

Lillian Smith donated a tall wooden stand with a large, gilded Bible to Glendale Church in memory of her daughter and husband who were tragically killed in a car accident. The stand had been placed at the front of the church, in the middle of the sanctuary, just beyond the altar railing. Previous ministers had adopted the habit of walking around it, or standing to the left or right of it to serve communion or give the benediction. But the new pastor, Pastor Callas, was an animated preacher, often pacing the floor during his sermons, and so he moved the stand over to the side prior to each Sunday service. But oddly, each time Pastor Callas came back to the sanctuary to begin the service, the stand had been moved back. His response was to move it back out of his way. After the service on his fourth Sunday, the lay leader pulled Pastor Callas aside and told him that they had gotten several complaints about the way he was conducting the service. Pastor Callas agreed to meet with some of the church's members to learn more. During this meeting a few people insisted that they just weren't used to "his style," but he also heard at least one person repeat that he "didn't like him moving that Bible stand."

"It has always been there," this man said, and his moving it was "disruptive."

Later Pastor Callas discovered the significance of the stand, and that Mrs. Smith had been terribly hurt by his moving it. In fact, it was she who had complained to the lay leader. Pastor Callas now had a decision to make. He could:

1. Stop moving the stand and make an adjustment in the way he delivered his sermons.
2. Go and talk with Mrs. Smith, apologize for not knowing the significance of the stand, and see if they could come up with a compromise.
3. Remind the church that he was in charge of the service, that this was his style of preaching, and that the stand was in his way. Furthermore, he could ask members to remember that their primary concern on Sunday should be with worshiping God and not with the placement of a stand.

All of these options are valid, but each will evoke a different response. Which option do you think Pastor Callas should choose? Take a minute to make your choice before you read on.

After a brief time of prayer, Pastor Callas called Mrs. Smith to ask if he could stop by for a visit. He did and shared with her that he had learned the significance of the stand, and he apologized for his insensitivity. He assured Mrs. Smith that he never meant to hurt her, then he invited her to tell him about her late husband and daughter. She opened a beautifully crafted photo album and shared her stories with Pastor Callas. Then before leaving, Pastor Callas turned to Mrs. Smith and said, "I won't move the stand anymore, and I'll try not to trip over it when preaching, but my pacing is such a bad habit. Will you keep me in your prayers?"

The following Sunday, Pastor Callas arrived to find that the stand had been moved against the wall to the right of the communion table. When Pastor Callas checked with the lay leader, he was told that Mrs. Smith had asked that the stand be moved, saying that she had found a better place for it. After the service, Pastor Callas asked Mrs. Smith if he could stop by that evening. He wanted to thank her. After that there were no more complaints about the way he was conducting the service.

Consider: Why do you think Pastor Callas chose this option? What were the benefits and the inherent risks of this option? What are some other ways Mrs. Smith could have responded?

# Example of Conflict Between Parishioners

When Porter Street Church's church council decided to host a concession booth at the County Fair, they had no idea that their sloppy joe stand would raise so much money. They raised $10,000. Prior to the fundraiser, they had agreed that they would give a portion of their profits to the community's food bank, but they had not discussed what else they would do with the money. After the fundraiser, the church council chairperson called a meeting to discuss how the money should be spent. Even though no more than fifteen members had worked the stand, and no more than twenty people were on the council, well over fifty people came to the meeting. Pastor Hartman was not the chair of the meeting, though she was a voting member of the council and so was present.

Even before the meeting started, it was apparent that the church had divided itself into two groups. One group, made up of younger members and a few church leaders, wanted to use the money to put in a new sound system and a video screen, so that the words to songs could be projected onto the screen, and graphics or films could be shown. Additionally, they wanted a CD and DVD player, so that they could buy contemporary music on CDs and have a way to show DVD movies for the youth. This was something that the church had discussed doing for several years to try to attract new and younger members. The other group was made up of some of the older members and several of the guardians. For years they had been wanting to remodel the sanctuary and refurbish the beautiful dark, cherry wood. They also felt the sanctuary needed new paint, new carpeting, and new pew cushions.

There was a great deal of tension in the room. Then to make matters worse, the chairperson called for a vote on how much they should set aside for the food pantry. Two of the members suggested $500, but others said no more than $100. After a heated discussion, the pastor decided to abstain from voting, but she reminded everyone that a faithful tithe to the food pantry would be $1,000 or 10 percent of the profit. Nonetheless, the committee voted, and the food pantry was allotted $100. By this time the meeting was disorderly. The younger people, in particular, who had worked at the concession stand, were angry that the older folks, who had not worked, were trying to control the agenda. Pastor Hartman needed to make a quick decision. What should she do?

1. Step in and try to quiet people down, then call for a written vote (with votes remaining confidential) to get a quick resolution so that the church could move forward.
2. Suggest that people put off voting until another time to give everyone a chance to calm down, then take the opportunity to remind people of the church's mission and emphasize that relationships and people are more important than paint or sound systems.
3. Step in as the voice of reason and suggest that each side prioritize their needs. Perhaps a new coat of paint and a sound system would be okay for now, then next year they could work toward getting enough money for the new carpet, a projection screen, and the DVD player.

While there are no absolute right or wrong answers here, some choices are better than others. If you have taken the time to get to know your community, its leaders, and its guardians, it will be easier to discern the best solution for your church.

Pastor Hartman asked the committee to postpone the vote for a later time. This gave her enough time to meet with some of the members on each side of the issue, get them to weigh one another's positions, and consider a compromise.

In the end the committee agreed that the preferences of the members who actually worked at the concession stand should be given priority. This group then chose to put in the new sound system and purchase the CD player. But they also agreed that it was important to protect all of the beautiful wood in the sanctuary, and so they set aside the rest of the money for the restoration. The church council then voted to do the fund raiser again the following year and said that any money made would be split between purchasing a projector and screen and painting the sanctuary. But to Pastor Hartman's dismay, they also voted that the food pantry would continue to receive no more than $100. In response she decided that she would do a sermon series on the importance of tithing and giving to missions.

# Example of Systemic Conflict

From his first week at West Side Church, Pastor Lee noticed his mostly middle-class, Caucasian congregation seemed to be racist. Visitors to the Sunday service from the surrounding neighborhood, which was mostly African American and Hispanic, were not welcomed with the same zeal with which white visitors were welcomed, if they were welcomed at all. Whenever Pastor Lee tried to get the church's members to greet these guests or acknowledge their presence, the members refused. But it wasn't until the church decided to hire a part-time youth minister, and two qualified African Americans from the neighborhood applied for the position, that the issue became an even more serious conflict. The church members ignored the applications of the two black applicants and instead voted to hire a friend of one of the church's leaders, a young white woman with no other credentials than that she was a college student and so a "youth" herself. Pastor Lee expressed concern to the church's leaders and guardians, yet they insisted that the decision to hire the young white woman was based upon her references and nothing more. So Pastor Lee set up an appointment to speak with a clergy mentor about his dilemma. The mentor asked Pastor Lee to come up with four possible responses to this situation, then they would meet again to discuss the options.

What four responses might you suggest? Let's look at Pastor Lee's list:

1. Confront the members with the evil of racism and remind them of their duty as Christians to welcome everyone in the name of Christ.
2. Offer a series of sermons and workshops on racism, and bring in local experts on the topic to whom this congregation might listen.
3. Invite an African American church choir to perform at a special service, such as a Thanksgiving or Christmas Eve service, or find other ways to expose this church to people of different races.
4. Invite the church's members to a special session. Share that as pastor you are concerned by what seems to be racist actions and give them a chance to explain, hoping that when they hear themselves talk about the issue, they will realize that they have a problem that needs to be addressed.

Together with his clergy mentor, Pastor Lee decided to hold a special meeting to discuss how guests are treated and who to hire as the church's new youth minister. He held the meeting in the fellowship hall, instead of the usual church council room, so that more people could attend, and so that people might feel more comfortable. The fellowship hall also helped make the point that the meeting was not "business as usual." Additionally, it gave him the space to set out some coffee and refreshments.

At this meeting he explained to the members that, though he loved this church dearly, there were some things that he didn't understand. If he was going to be a good leader, he needed their help. So before they officially hired any youth minister, he asked them to help him better understand why this community makes the decisions that it makes.

To begin, Pastor Lee welcomed the members, thanked them for their willingness to attend, then posed a question, "Can you help me understand your attitude toward visitors? Do you like visitors? Or do you feel that the church is just the right size and you don't really want new members?"

At first everyone said that they "loved visitors," and that they were a "friendly and welcoming congregation."

Pastor Lee responded, "Without putting any of our newer members on the spot, is this how you first experienced our church, as warm and friendly?"

Gradually some of the newer members began to share that they hadn't felt especially welcome at first. "This seems to be a tight-knit congregation, which can be good, but this also makes it kind of hard to break into," one new member said. Many of the older members seemed surprised and even shocked to hear this, but Pastor Lee noticed that they *were* listening.

After some discussion, Pastor Lee shared his particular concern over the hiring of the youth minister. "I am not accusing anyone of anything, I just want to hear more about how you arrived at the decision."

Initial responses focused on the fact that the white girl and her family were friends with someone in the congregation. "Okay, maybe she wasn't necessarily the *most* qualified," one longtime member said. "But shouldn't we hire someone who has a connection to our congregation?"

Then a new member spoke up, "Could the reason that we didn't hire the black applicants be because they are black?"

A guardian quickly answered, "We've been accused of being racist before. But I work with blacks and have neighbors who are blacks, so that's not the problem."

"Then why weren't the black applicants considered?" Pastor Lee asked.

Another longtime member answered, "Pastor, this church was built eighty-three years ago because a group of us from this neighborhood were not welcome at that church down the street. They thought they were too good for us. They were the 'rich folks' and they didn't want factory workers in their church. So a bunch of us from this neighborhood got together and formed our own church and were eventually able to build this building. My mother was the church's first women's group leader. But over the years the neighborhood changed. The houses were torn down. Apartments went up. Stores moved out. Other people moved in. Lower-class people. And we don't want *them* to come in here and change *us*. It happens that many of them are minorities. But it doesn't really matter what color they are, we just don't want those people coming in and making changes."

With this answer, Pastor Lee confirmed that the church had a problem, but a different problem than what he had first thought. Yet the special meeting had given him the opportunity to better position himself as a member of this community, a member who was willing to listen and work *with* them. Pastor Lee was now in a stronger position to help members overcome their fear and reach out to others, all the while knowing that there was no guarantee that he would be successful.

One of the most important things to remember when dealing with systematic conflict is that you never want to become isolated or to make the conflict into a situation where it becomes the pastor versus the church. And it is best not to set up the conflict as win or lose. There is rarely a winner in conflict, only opportunities for people to grow or not to grow. Because of this, Pastor Lee decided not to push the matter further at the meeting and *make* the members hire one of the black applicants. Though he might have gotten the votes, he also knew that the church was not yet prepared to welcome an outsider as their youth minister.

As pastor, you always want to present your church members with opportunities to grow in their faith. This means that sometimes you will need to encourage them as they begin to take baby steps toward a more faithful life. At other times you must support them as they risk taking giant leaps forward.

Unfortunately, there will also be times when you encounter a congregation who refuses to change or grow: the systemic problems are too engrained. If you find yourself at such a church, spend a lot of time in prayer and discernment so that you can make the best decision for you: to stay or to look for a call to another church. Whatever the decision, be sure that there are opportunities for *you* to continue to grow and move forward, even if your church chooses not to do so.

# Pastor's Checklist

Stay prepared for conflict, but do not expect conflict to lurk around every corner. Instead, build strong relationships with all of the people in your parish, learn as much as you can about the history of your parish and its people, and look for opportunities to practice and improve your conflict negotiation skills. Periodically review the list below.

# Rules for Negotiating Conflict

1. Can you state the conflict? Write it down and try to summarize it in one paragraph. This will help to clarify the issue at hand, not only for yourself but for all parties involved.

2. Do members involved in the conflict have an accurate understanding of both sides of the issue? Can you state what each person or each side wants, their particular goals, and their motivation? Can they?

3. Check your emotions and keep your emotions in check. Heightened emotions will keep you from thinking clearly. While emotions can serve to inform you, make sure that you do not let your emotions guide your actions. Don't be afraid to stop, step back, and take a deep breath. Ask others to do so too.

4. Remember, conflict is rarely about you, the pastor. Although members might present the conflict as one that came with you, most church conflicts have been around for a long time.

5. Style matters. Stay calm, speak with an even-toned voice, and make sure your gestures are nonthreatening (e.g., don't point at someone). Also, restate negative sentences in the positive. For example, "It sounds like we are choosing between two good things. We've been blessed with $10,000 to spend, and so either choice, whether we buy a new sound system or remodel the sanctuary, will be a good thing for this church and for this community."

6. Make sure that your response is equal in proportion to the conflict. Just as you would not ground your son for six months for accidentally spilling a glass of milk or simply ignore a daughter who was self-destructive, don't overreact or underreact to situations in the church.

7. Make sure each side can accurately articulate the history of the conflict. Sometimes people fight when they do not know what they are fighting about. Also be attentive to the history of the relationships involved in the conflict. Sometimes people fight about one thing when what is really bothering them is something else.

8. Consider which side holds the most influence in the conflict and why. But take care not to be cooped by the more powerful members simply because this seems like the path of least resistance.

9. Can you state the expectations of each party in the conflict? Can they? What are the consequences of "winning" or "losing" this conflict? Can there be a clear "winner" or "loser"? Can you make a list of all of the possible outcomes? How many outcomes might be appealing or acceptable?

10. Is there something that one side has that can be traded with the other? Can this be solved by both sides giving up something they have or want in order to gain something they may want more? If there is no clear solution, work for a compromise that satisfies both sides. If the parties can't reach an agreement, are there any other alternatives? If so, what are they?

Ministers of all faiths report having a positive experience with the Alban Institute. The Alban Institute is an ecumenical, interfaith organization founded in 1974 that supports congregations and clergy through consulting services, research, book publishing, Web site material, and educational seminars. Particularly known for expertise in congregational conflict, their consultants and mediators are equipped to work with you through a wide range of difficult situations and circumstances. To visit the Alban Institute's Web site go to http://www.alban.org. Or contact them at: The Alban Institute, Suite 100, 2121 Cooperative Way, Herndon, VA 20171; (703) 964-2700, (800) 486-1318, webmaster@alban.org.

# CHAPTER SEVEN

# DRAFT A PLAN FOR YOUR CHURCH

When Ron Delaney arrived at his first church, he was ready to put into practice all that he had learned in school. Christ the King was a small, inner-city church, but it hadn't always been small. About twenty years ago the church was located in what was then an expanding section of the city, and the pews were filled each Sunday. But over time the area was hit hard economically, and year by year church membership dwindled.

So when Pastor Delaney arrived, he quickly realized that the church's problem was that it did not know how to reach out to the surrounding neighborhood. Ron had always had a particular concern for animals, and he noticed that there was an animal shelter overflowing with unwanted dogs and cats just down the street from the church. So he presented a proposal to the church's governing counsel to partner with the shelter and help them create a foster program. The basic idea was that members of the church would take some of the adoptable animals from the shelter into their homes until permanent owners could be found. Additionally, the church would work with the shelter by advertising the animals and sponsoring adoption days. Pastor Delaney believed that since the church and the shelter shared a similar problem—being invisible to the larger community—that they'd make natural partners.

The employees at the shelter embraced Pastor Delaney's idea, and several even expressed an interest in attending Christ the King. But the leaders at Christ the King were decidedly less enthusiastic. Their initial response was, "We've never done anything like this before. It'll never work."

But Pastor Delaney persisted. He responded to the members' concerns and explained how the foster plan would work and how it could benefit the church by attracting new members—not to mention saving the lives of the animals. "Yes, it will be a learning experience," he told them, "and we'll make mistakes, but it will be easier once we practice it." At first, committee meetings to discuss the issue were long and argumentative, but eventually a majority seemed to agree and voted to give the foster program a try.

Things went well for the first few months, though only a handful of members volunteered to help. But several of the shelter's employees were now attending or had joined the church, and they, along with Christ the King's volunteers, were rescuing about half a dozen animals a month. Yet several of the church's long-time members had not given up their resistance. Whenever a problem arose, however minor, they exaggerated its impact. Furthermore, they made the visitors and new members from the shelter feel unwelcome. Although the animal out-reach program remained for as long as Pastor Delaney was their minister, as soon as he left Christ the King, the church voted to discontinue the program.

With this experience behind him, Pastor Delaney decided to try a different approach at his second church, New Hope Church. He now knew that it was more important to develop a plan *with* a local church than to develop a plan *for* it. He had discovered that it is only when a congregation feels a personal sense of ownership in a ministry that it will have long-term success. So Pastor Delaney made it a priority at New Hope Church to help the members discover what ministry *they* wanted to undertake.

# An Overview of the Planning Process

This chapter will walk you through a sample planning process, using Pastor Delaney as an example. It begins at New Hope Church with a one-day retreat for leaders and other members of the congregation. It illustrates how a pastor can encourage a church to find its mission, and then to set some concrete goals to implement its mission over the coming year. The chapter then concludes with some tips a pastor can use to prepare the congregation for change.

The goal of the one-day planning retreat is twofold: (1) to have the participants reflect upon the universal mission of the Church, and (2) to have them develop a particular, local ministry statement for their congregation. (Note: for the purposes of this chapter, when *Church* begins with a capital letter, it refers to Christ's universal Church as it has existed throughout the ages, whereas *church* with a small "c" refers to a particular local congregation.)

Pastor Delaney, for example, began the retreat at New Hope by challenging members to distinguish between the mission of the Church universal, which applies to all Christians everywhere, and the local ministry statement of a particular church, which is contextual. Both are important, but they are distinct. All churches are supposed to have the same general mission, but they embody this mission differently, and so actual ministries will vary from congregation to congregation. *A local ministry statement highlights the identity of a particular church and suggests a certain plan of action for that specific church.*

For example, while the mission statement of the Church universal is summed up by Jesus in Matthew 22:37-38 in the Great Commandment—love God and neighbor—and in Matthew 28:19-20 in the Great Commission—make disciples of all nations—a local ministry statement might be "a traditional Episcopal service that welcomes all." The latter statement identifies the uniqueness of *a particular church*: it comes from the Anglican tradition, has retained a liturgical and sacramental style of worship, and yet is willing to embrace a diverse mix of people in its congregation.

Some congregations will already have a clear sense of the Church's mission and a relatively good local ministry statement when you arrive, but even so, planning retreats is still a good idea, especially at the beginning of a new pastorate. Just as you were asked in chapter 1 to write a personal ministry statement to give focus to your new ministry, it is important to give each new church that you serve a chance to revisit and revise its ministry statement, if they have one, or if they don't have one, the opportunity to write their own.

Furthermore, a planning retreat gives you the opportunity to build a base of support and gives both you and the congregation a chance to get to know each other.

# A Sample Planning Retreat

Pastor Delaney waited to schedule the planning retreat until after he had been at the church for at least three months, because he wanted a chance to establish some relationships and learn everyone's name. Then he sent individual invitations to church leaders and issued a general invitation to its members in the newsletter. Because it offered a more relaxed and creative environment, he decided to hold the retreat at a nearby retreat center, as opposed to the church. He felt this would be a nice alternative to meeting in the church's fellowship hall. He also requested RSVP's so that he'd know how many people to expect, and he asked members to bring their Bibles and a brown bag lunch.

The retreat was scheduled for a Saturday beginning at 8:30 A.M., and Pastor Delaney had set out a light continental breakfast ahead of time. At 9:00 A.M. he led the people in an opening song, "We Are the Church," followed by an opening prayer. He then passed around copies of the agenda for the morning. Obviously, dates and times can be modified to fit the context of your retreat:

Planning Retreat Schedule
    8:30 A.M.: Gathering and Continental Breakfast

9:00 A.M.: Welcome and Opening Song "We Are the Church"
Opening Prayer
Overview of the Morning
Guidelines for Group Discussion (See handout at end of chapter.)

9:30 A.M.: "The Church's Mission Statement"
Exercise One: Divide into Small Groups for Discussion of Various Christian Activities (20 min.) (See handout at end of chapter.)
Reconvene for Large Group Discussion (20 min.)
Exercise Two: Divide into Small Groups for Discussion of the Church's Timeless Mission (10 min.) (See handout at end of chapter.)
Reconvene for Large Group Discussion (10 min.)

10:30 A.M.: Break

10:45 A.M.: "Our Local Ministry Statement"
Exercise Three: Divide into Small Groups for Discussion of Our Particular Strengths (20 min.) (See handout at end of chapter.)
Reconvene for Large Group Discussion (20 min.)
Exercise Four: Divide into Small Groups for Discussion of Our Local Ministry Statement (10 min.) (See handout at end of chapter.)
Reconvene for Large Group Discussion (10 min.)

11:45 A.M.: Break Time

Noon: Worship and Holy Communion followed by brown bag lunch
Retreat to end around 12:30 P.M.

As Pastor Delaney went over the agenda, he shared that the purpose of the retreat was to explore the mission of the universal Church and to develop a particular ministry statement for New Hope. "Most of our day," he said, "will involve discussions either together in this room or in small groups. To make sure everyone feels comfortable participating, let's go over some guidelines." (See the "Planning Retreat Handout—Guidelines for Group Discussions" at the end of the chapter.)

# Reflecting upon the Church's Mission

Pastor Delaney explained that they would spend the first half of the retreat exploring the scriptural understanding of the Church's mission. He quickly divided the large group into small groups of three or more members and let each group choose where to meet: various empty rooms in the retreat center or places outside nearby. He suggested that each group select a leader by identifying the person whose birthday came next. "The group leader's responsibility is to take notes and to report back to the larger group," he explained. Then he handed out the first set of questions for each group to discuss. "You'll have twenty minutes to go over the questions, then please return and rejoin the larger group," Pastor Delaney said before dismissing them to do the exercise. (See "Planning Retreat Handout—Exercise One: Various Christian Activities" at the end of the chapter.)

Once the small groups had discussed the various kinds of activities that are found in healthy, faithful churches and had returned to the larger group, Pastor Delaney asked each small group leader to name the activity his or her group chose as the *most important* one. Pastor Delaney listed the answers up front on a flip chart so that everyone could see.

After each group leader had a chance to share at least one idea, he opened the floor for further discussion: "What other activities were discussed in your groups?" "Have we left out anything important that Christians should be doing on a regular basis?" Pastor Delaney listed the additional ideas on the chart, even if they were similar to the ones that had already been shared. He also tried to list the suggestions exactly as they were worded, shortening them only as space on the flip chart required.

Eventually Pastor Delaney had a good, long list:

> worship
> pray
> love God
> love neighbor
> read the Bible
> visit one another
> invite people to church
> feed the hungry
> help those less fortunate
> take care of the building
> care for animals and creation
> teach children about God
> celebrate communion

"Now," Pastor Delaney said, "let's put similar items together. In other words, can you find the ideas that would naturally fit together within a common category?"

Here's what the New Hope members suggested:

| Category 1 | Category 2 | Category 3 |
|---|---|---|
| worship | pray | visit one another |
| love God | read the Bible | love neighbor |
| communion | | invite people to church |
| | | feed the hungry |
| | | help those less fortunate |
| | | care for animals and creation |

Uncertain about where to list "teach children about God," they decided to put it under both the first *and* second category. They also weren't sure where to put "take care of building" so they set it aside for the time being.

Next, Pastor Delaney drew a circle or "bucket" around each category and explained the bucket concept: that the next task was to label or come up with a title for each category or "bucket."

Together they decided to label the first category or bucket "church activities," the second, "spirituality," and the third, "missions." A final category was then added and labeled "miscellaneous," in which they placed "take care of building."

Note: Every church will have a slightly different set of ideas, and thus a different number of categories, as well as their own labels. This is fine. In the end, however, the most common types of groupings usually involve (1) worship (e.g., prayer), (2) study (e.g., Bible study), (3) fellowship (e.g., pot lucks), (4) service (e.g., helping at a food pantry), and (5) evangelism (e.g., inviting others to church).

"For the next step in this process," Pastor Delaney said, "I'd like to invite you to return to your small groups. Now that you have identified the main types of activities that are important in every church and have labeled them *church activities, spirituality, missions,* and *miscellaneous,* can you use these general themes to come up with one statement that captures the essential mission of the Church? In other words, what I want your small groups to do next is to write a sentence or statement in everyday language that states the mission of Christ's Church. You'll have ten minutes to do this. Once you're done, you can return again to the large group." (See "Planning Retreat Handout—Exercise Two: The Church's Timeless Mission" at the end of the chapter.)

After they had returned, Pastor Delaney asked each small group leader to share his or her sentence or statement. One statement read, "Christians should go to church, read the Bible, pray, and help those in need." Another read, "Christians come together to worship God and to grow spiritually so that they can be a blessing to others." A third stated, "The church is a place where God acts to save individuals and through them make a difference in the world." And a fourth was "We are a community called by Christ to grow in holiness and witness to God's presence in the world."

After writing all of the statements up front on the flip chart, Pastor Delaney stepped back and asked them to notice how similar they were, despite the different wordings. He opened the Bible and read aloud a couple of the mission statements from the list of Scripture passages distributed earlier (on the handout for exercise one), and noted the similar themes of nurture and outreach contained in them all. "This completes the first part of our retreat today, and I want to congratulate you on your work so far," Pastor Delaney said. "But we are not done yet."

# Developing a Congregational Ministry Statement

"Many churches spend hours arriving at nicely crafted mission statements like we've just done," Pastor Delaney continued. "The statements are true, but they are not necessarily useful for guiding a local church's ministry. Therefore, the goal of the second part of this morning is to develop a particular ministry statement for New Hope Church. The ministry statement will have to be consistent with the above mission, which is why we began by talking about what all churches have in common, but our ministry statement will differ from the previous mission statement by highlighting the unique way in which the Church's timeless mission is embodied here at New Hope. Before we do that, though, let's all take a fifteen-minute break. We'll reconvene here at 10:45 A.M."

After the break, Pastor Delaney asked the members to return to their small groups and follow the same format as before, only with a different set of questions. "This second set of questions," he explained, "is designed to bring out what is uniquely Christian about New Hope Church. As you did with the first set of questions, discuss them for twenty minutes and then rejoin the larger group." (See "Planning Retreat Handout—Exercise Three: Our Particular Strengths" at the end of the chapter.)

Once the small groups completed this exercise and returned to the large group, Pastor Delaney followed the same procedure as before. He asked each small group leader, one at a time, for his or her answer. He listed the answers up front so that everyone could see them, and after each group had had a chance to share at least one idea, he opened the floor for further discussion. "In terms of the questions on the handout, what other strengths were discussed? What else are we passionate about at New Hope that guests might also find interesting?"

These new passions were listed along with the others. Some of the things included were:

- Our new food pantry and its opportunities to help out those less fortunate
- Our Sunday school classes for children, including our goal to start some new ones
- Our contemporary service on Sunday and our Wednesday night service
- Our Wednesday night youth group
- Raising money for the local children's orphanage
- Supporting a mission trip to Haiti each year
- Learning and singing contemporary worship songs

Once all the ideas were listed, Pastor Delaney again had them engage in the "bucket" exercise: "Is there a label we could put on each bucket that might serve to describe the ideas that we've listed and sorted?"

They eventually came up with two categories:

Category 1: Outreach
missions
food pantry
children's home
Haiti trip

Category 2: Nurture
church meetings
children's Sunday school
new contemporary service
new Wednesday night service
Wednesday night youth group
singing

Pastor Delaney then went over the last handout and sent them back one last time to their small groups for discussion. This time each group would come up with a suggested ministry statement for New Hope Church, and each group leader would take a sheet from the flip chart and write the statement on the sheet so that everyone could read it once he or she returned to the large group. (See "Planning Retreat Handout—Exercise Four: Our Local Ministry Statement" at the end of the chapter.)

Pastor Delaney gave the small groups about ten minutes to write their statements, and then asked them to return. Once they did, he invited each group to share its statement, and he hung up the flip sheets so that everyone else could see them.

Suggested statements included:

- "We are a small church who actively reaches out to the community."
- "We are an informal group who worship God in a variety of settings, and try to share the love of God with others."
- "Joined by our worship of Jesus, we extend our hospitality to people regardless of income or nationality."
- "We offer opportunities to put your faith into practice."

"Let's compare the various statements," Pastor Delaney said. "Does anyone see a common vision emerging?"

As the entire group now worked together to draft a common vision statement for New Hope's ministry, Pastor Delaney asked them to keep in mind the last two questions on the worksheet: What qualities *ought to* characterize a member of New Hope Church? What kind of church do we want *our church* to be?

Pastor Delaney discovered that one of the things people liked about New Hope Church was its small size. They were glad that the church was growing, but still they liked the fact that everyone knew each other. They also discovered during the discussion that, even though they were a small church, they still had something unique to offer the larger community. Most small churches are not as involved in as many mission projects as New Hope. And while larger churches have more money for mission projects, they don't have the same small-family feeling. New Hope Church is unique, they realized, because they are a small church with a variety of hands-on opportunities for Christian mission.

# The End of the Retreat: Where We Go from Here

"I intend to save all of the statements and edit them into one ministry statement that can be presented to the governing council for further discussion and possible adoption back at the church," Pastor Delaney told the group as they prepared for worship. "The goal of our retreat was not to arrive at a final edited statement, but I think we have an excellent first draft." The finished statement that New Hope eventually adopted read, *We are a small Christian church, who invites everyone to join us in our contemporary worship of Christ, as we seek to fulfill Christ's call to reach out to others with compassion.*

Pastor Delaney then used the remainder of the retreat to start setting some possible goals for the next year. "Given the draft of our ministry statement, what are some ways over the next year that we might strengthen our small family feel while extending our outreach ministries?"

The members quickly offered their ideas:

- "Could we have a Christmas party for our food pantry clients?"
- "I'd like to get children involved in choir and music."
- "Could we have a fund-raising dinner along with our craft and bake sale, and maybe use some of the money for the Haiti trip?"
- "I'd like to get some new decorations for our sanctuary—something more contemporary for the new service."

"Those are excellent ideas," Pastor Delaney said. "I'm writing them down so that we can discuss them later, back at the church." He then closed the retreat with Holy Communion followed by the brown bag lunch.

# Set Specific Goals and Develop a Plan of Action

As Pastor Delaney worked with his various committees to follow up on the ideas mentioned at the retreat and to set specific goals for the church for the following year, he handed out the "Setting Goals" sheet and asked the members to keep its criteria in mind as they worked through its questions. (See "Setting Goals" at the end of the chapter.)

For example, at the next meeting of the church's mission committee, Pastor Delaney told them that one part of New Hope's ministry statement read "to reach out to others with compassion." Although New Hope was already doing a good job through their food pantry and mission trip to Haiti, money was tight. They knew that they could do even more if they had more money feed more people or take another person on the Haiti trip. And so Pastor Delaney told them that one of the ideas mentioned at the New Hope retreat was to hold a fund raising dinner with the annual craft and bake sale. This dinner was something that hadn't been considered before. It also addressed a current weakness of their craft and bake sale: it attracted the same crowd year after year. The dinner might bring new people to the craft sale, as well as serve the secondary purpose of giving the church members another activity that families could participate in together.

The mission committee agreed to ask the members who planned the craft sale if they could add a fund-raising dinner. After they did this, and once everyone agreed to the dinner, a task force was formed to break down the dinner into manageable tasks: select the meal, advertise, serve and clean up afterwards, and so on. After they worked out a timetable and budget, they decided to meet at some point after the dinner to assess how it went, and how, if they were to do it again, they could improve it in the future.

# Tips on Sharing the New Vision with the Congregation

The members at New Hope were genuinely open to change and trying new things. If your church is eager for change, it might be possible to make a number of changes fairly quickly. In fact, if your church is expecting change, it is best to make it a priority. But if your church, like so many churches, is resistant to change, proceed with caution.

People resist change for a variety of reasons: they fear failure, they are comfortable with the status quo, they feel left out of the process, they do not like the person suggesting the change, change is hard work, and the unknown is frightening. Even in the healthiest of churches, some people will refuse to accept changes, but that said, there are things you can do to make transitions easier:

1. Do not try to change too much too fast. When changing one thing, make sure that other things remain the same, and start with small changes that have immediate results that can be seen or quantified.

2. Affirm the past history of the church at every opportunity. In fact, some changes are best presented as recovering traditions. For example, before you introduce guitar music into the worship service, remind members of how they have loved having special music in previous years.

3. Provide numerous opportunities for people to discuss a specific change, even after the change has taken place. Don't assume that just because people voted for a change one week, that they'll still be supportive of it a month later.

4. Pay special attention to anyone who is resistant to the change. If members feel that you truly care about them and their feelings, they might take the changes less personally.

5. Introduce any changes as provisional. "We'll try this for six months and see how it works. If it doesn't work, we can always go back to how things were."

6. Remind people how each change is an attempt to live out the Church's universal mission and the particular ministry focus they have chosen.

7. Celebrate every small change and give the credit for its success to the congregation.

Remember, a pastor's job is to share the church's vision with the entire congregation through preaching, Bible study, the newsletter, and to support the congregation in living out their mission, ministry, and plan of action. And while it is not the pastor's job to do everything by himself or herself, when a pastor and congregation see themselves as members of the same team, much can be accomplished.

# Pastor's Checklist

1. Print your church's ministry statement on all newsletters, bulletins, flyers, brochures, stationery, advertisements, etc.

2. Churches are never static, but are always changing. Where is your congregation growing? Where is it dying? To find answers ask: Where is the energy? Where is the highest level of commitment? What programs in this church are successful and run smoothly? Or the opposite: Where is the least amount of energy? Where is there conflict, resistance, or a lack of support or trust?

3. When making changes, watch for subtle signs of resistance. Members sometimes use nonverbal communication to let you know they are unhappy. Look for anyone who resigns a post, stops volunteering, or

attending meetings. Chronic lateness, especially from members who used to show up early or on time, a reduction of giving, acts of vandalism or theft, a drop in worship attendance, and conflict over seemingly trivial matters all signal trouble.

4. When *can* a pastor suggest a new idea or start a new program? A good time to suggest new ideas is after you have been at the church for at least six months and are 95 percent certain that a new program will have the support of the majority of the congregation. Additionally, the change must fit well with the church's ministry statement and be within the church's means.

5. Whenever a church tries something new, look for new leaders to emerge. If a member is particularly excited about an idea, find out if he or she would make a good leader for that project.

6. Familiarize yourself with the dynamics of change and growth: organizations such as the Center for Parish Development, Net Workshops, Fred Pryor/Career Track, and the Alban Institute all offer pamphlets, books, study materials, and workshops on how to successfully initiate change and growth.

# PLANNING RETREAT HANDOUT

## Guidelines for Group Discussions

1. <u>No editing. No criticizing.</u> Today we will be listing and categorizing different ideas. Remember, there are no wrong answers. We are not critiquing each other's ideas; instead, we are brainstorming. One idea might trigger a thought or insight for someone else, and this is an important process, so please, no interruptions.

2. <u>Encourage one another</u>. Whenever someone offers a thought or insight, give positive feedback:
   a. "Good!"
   b. "Wow! That makes me think of another idea!"
   c. "Keep going! You're doing great!"

3. If you don't have an idea, <u>be a cheerleader</u>. If you are not a good cheerleader, smile and nod, or offer thoughtful silence while someone jots the idea down.

4. <u>Weirdness, zaniness, humor, and pie-in-the-sky are welcomed and encouraged</u>. Creativity is more likely to occur in an atmosphere of uninhibited fun.

5. <u>Focus on the goal</u>. We are searching for something intangible and exciting. Our ultimate quest is not for a marketing slogan, but to identify the heart and soul of our Christian life together. The broader, farther, and deeper we are willing to go with our thoughts and suggestions, the better.

6. <u>Just for today assume money is not an object</u>. Our goal is to arrive at a vision. So if you think it's important that we build a meditation garden with a reflecting pool, then say so.

7. <u>Share the credit</u>. Because crafting a mission statement is a shared process, credit for the end result belongs to everybody. We are a team, and today everyone is an important part of the process.

# PLANNING RETREAT HANDOUT

## Exercise One: Various Christian Activities

1. What kinds of activities can be found in a healthy, faithful church? In other words, what sorts of things should Christians be doing in the church and in the world? (Examples might include praying for people, attending worship, or participating in Bible study.)

2. Of the various answers to question 1, which one would you list as the most important?

3. As you answer question 2, consider how the Bible answers the question. What did Jesus do while he was here? What did he tell his followers to do? What did the first churches do? The following scriptural passages are a good place to start: Matthew 5:13-16 (You are the salt of the earth); 10:5-14 (The Mission of the Twelve); 11:28-30 (Come to me, all you that are weary); 16:13-19 (Peter's declaration about Jesus); 18:20-21 (Forgiveness); 22:36-40 (Love God and Neighbor); 25:34-40 (Judgment of the Nations); 28:16-20 (The Commissioning of the Disciples); Mark 10:43-45 (Not to rule, but to serve); Luke 4:16-21 (Jesus in Nazareth); John 13:34-35 (A new command: to love); 20:30-31 (Signs leading to belief); Acts 1:8 (Witnesses to all the Earth); 2:1-13 (The Day of Pentecost); 2:41-47, 4:32-37, and 5:42 (Life among the believers); and Romans 12:1-21 (New Life in Christ).

# PLANNING RETREAT HANDOUT

## Exercise Two: The Church's Timeless Mission

Take a look at the following list of Scripture readings again:

Matthew 5:13-16 (You are the salt of the earth); 10:5-14 (The Mission of the Twelve); 11:28-30 (Come to me, all you that are weary); 16:13-19 (Peter's declaration about Jesus); 18:20-21 (Forgiveness); 22:36-40 (Love God and Neighbor); 25:34-40 (Judgment of the Nations); 28:16-20 (The Commissioning of the Disciples); Mark 10:43-45 (Not to rule, but to serve); Luke 4:16-21 (Jesus in Nazareth); John 13:34-35 (A new command: to love); 20:30-31 (Signs leading to belief); Acts 1:8 (Witnesses to all the Earth); 2:1-13 (The Day of Pentecost); 2:41-47, 4:32-37, and 5:42 (Life among the believers); and Romans 12:1-21 (New Life in Christ).

What are some of the examples of mission statements in the above passages?

Think about the mission statements found in the Bible. Also consider categories of Christian activities that we came up with in Exercise One. Can you state, in everyday language, how you would describe the timeless mission of Christ's Church? Imagine that you are describing the Church's mission to someone who has never read the Bible, and so try not to use religious words that might not have a clear and concrete meaning to someone not raised in the Church. Write your mission statement below:

# Planning Retreat Handout

## Exercise Three: Our Particular Strengths

To the public at large: You should come to our church instead of all the other churches in town because here you can experience a unique transformation.

1. This is true because our church emphasizes (list various things below)

As you answer question 1, consider the following:

2. When it comes to Christianity at this church, we are most passionate about

3. Our main strengths are

4. If we were to shut our doors tomorrow, the world would be missing out on

# Planning Retreat Handout

## Exercise Four: Our Local Ministry Statement

Write a ministry statement for our church: What common theme (or set of themes) ties together all of the activities, strengths, and passions that we have discussed? That is, your task is to write a particular ministry statement to sum up the unique ministry of our church: either what it is now or what you want it to be.

As you consider your statement, think about what qualities ought to characterize a member of our church, as well as what kind of church we want our church to be.

Below are a few samples of good and bad ministry statements:

1. "We are called to be fishers of humankind." While this is true of all churches, it is too vague. It doesn't tell us this church's *particular* vision.
2. "Let's just praise the Lord!" Although this comes from a holiness church that does emphasize praising God, it is still too general in that it could apply to any church.
3. "Bringing Christ to the Millennium Generation through contemporary worship." This statement is good in that it identifies something unique about the church—their intended audience and what their worship is like. But do they do anything besides worship God in a contemporary style?
4. "We are a Lutheran congregation, with members from various backgrounds and nationalities, that seeks to grow closer to God through the regular celebration of Christ's sacraments and by reaching out to the poor in the world." This statement is good in that it identifies who they are—a diverse mix of "high church" Lutherans—and what they see as their primary mission or task—sharing God's love with those less fortunate.

The best ministry statement will lend itself to developing a plan of action and setting specific goals for the church in the next year. A useful ministry statement must be honest. For example, if a congregation has no passion about starting a soup kitchen, their ministry statement shouldn't talk about feeding the hungry.

What ministry statement does your group suggest? Write it below:

# Setting Goals

A Good Goal:

• Is one that is concrete, specific, and reflects our church's particular ministry statement.
• Will be realistic and fit within the church's present context.
• Will have a broad base of support in the congregation.
• Will be measurable, so that we can know if the goal is being met.

Remember:

• A few good goals are better than many mediocre ones.
• Large goals should be broken down into smaller steps.
• Initial goals should be small and achievable, leading to quick victories that have immediate payoffs.

How to set a goal:

1. Before setting specific goals, decide what part of the ministry statement we want to address. That is, what larger purpose are we trying to accomplish with these specific goals? (All goals need to be in harmony with the particular ministry statement of the local congregation, as well as with the general mission of the Christ's universal Church.)

2. Current Situation: In terms of question 1, where are we right now?
   Strengths: What are we already doing well?
   Weaknesses: Where do we need more work?
   Opportunities: Are there some opportunities that we've been ignoring?
   Obstacles: What is the greatest obstacle or threat keeping us from achieving our larger purpose?

3. What specific goals can we set to help us become more faithful and fruitful in our ministry? How will these particular goals help us better achieve our larger purpose and mission?

How to implement a goal:

1. Which of our goals need to be broken down into smaller parts, and who is going to do each task? What is the timetable for these actions? Who is responsible for monitoring and coordinating the effort? What might go wrong, and how could we respond if it does?

2. Budget: What will each idea cost in terms of time, money, and human resources?

3. Assessment: How will we evaluate our efforts, so that we can learn from our successes and failures?

# CHAPTER EIGHT

# CREATE OPPORTUNITIES FOR FELLOWSHIP, STUDY, AND COMMUNITY

Seaside Church is a brand new church in a growing coastal community. It was formed by local residents who were seeking to distinguish themselves from the growing number of tourists, shopkeepers, and innkeepers who serve as part-time, summer residents. The initial group of fifteen members began meeting in homes for Bible study, but they quickly grew, split into two groups, then expanded until they rented a building and became a church. Now Seaside Church has approximately 100 members of different ages and races.

The Reverend Lucas Stevens, a young man in his late twenties, was just chosen to be the pastor. Just out of divinity school, Pastor Stevens is excited about the challenge, but is anxious too, because he knows that it is his responsibility to organize this church, design its programming, choose its style of worship, and set the rituals that will hopefully build Seaside into a strong, faithful, and productive community.

## Essential Events for Every Church

All churches need at least three different kinds of events if they want to be healthy and grow: *Come Level events, Explore Level events,* and *Grow Level events.* Let's take a look at each type:

At *Come Level events,* little is expected of participants. Sunday worship is an example. Anyone should be able to come to the Sunday worship service and, other than not being disruptive, nothing more should be expected or required. Other examples of Come Level events are concerts, movies, special services, lectures, plays, or a church bazaar. At a healthy church, the majority of the events will be Come Level events and will usually attract at least 60 percent of the congregation.

At *Explore Level events,* classes or meetings provide opportunities for people to explore their faith, possibilities for them to make new friends, and prospects for them to join the community. Explore Level events can be anything from Sunday school classes and Bible studies, to small group meetings, to a movie night with a discussion afterwards, to a potluck dinner, to a special interest group, such as a men's group or a quilting circle. Participation at the Explore Level is always greater than at the Come Level because some interaction and fellowship is expected. A healthy church can anticipate that at least 30 percent of the congregation will attend events at this level.

At *Grow Level events,* commitment is expected, participation and some level of accountability is required, and confidentiality is usually discussed. The goal of Grow Level events is for the participants to grow in their faith, in their relationships with others, as well as in their relationship with God. Pastoral counseling is a Grow Level event, as is a specialized workshop or seminar, leadership training classes, spiritual retreats and conferences, a focused study (such as a study group that does an eight-week program), a particular mission or outreach program (for example, a group that volunteers at a homeless shelter), marriage counseling, spiritual direction, or a grief support group. At least 10 percent of the community in a healthy church will be actively seeking to grow in their faith.

Some pastors mistakenly think that their goal should be to move members from Come Level to Explore Level to Grow Level, and if the church does not continually have more people at the Explore Level or Grow Level events, it is somehow failing. But this is not true. While everyone should be invited, even encouraged, to move from Come Level to Explore Level to Grow Level, the reality is that Come Level events will always have the highest attendance, while Explore Level and Grow Level combined will remain a minority, and this is as it should be. Notice, however, that larger crowds at Come Level events mean more opportunities for the other two levels to increase in numbers.

But, you might ask, if Grow Level events attract only 10 percent of the congregation, does this mean that the majority of people will never explore their faith or grow? No, it does not. Maturity, personalities, time schedules, other commitments, cultural influences, and so forth, all go into determining who attends what events at your church. A single father who is sincere about his faith and his relationship with God, but who works double shifts, may only attend Sunday worship with his children. However, a wise pastor will want to identify such people, visit them, and invite them to consider one Explore Level or Grow Level event, but not expect them to commit to much more.

Alternatively, a shy single woman in her mid-forties may have a free schedule, but may not feel comfortable in small group settings and so will only attend events where she can be a member of a crowd. She will show up for Come Level events, and she may go with the group that serves the monthly meal at the homeless shelter, a Grow Level event, but she will never attend a Sunday school class (Explore Level). In contrast, a person who likes to participate in small groups, but detests crowds, may be a faithful member of a Sunday school class but will never attend a Sunday worship service.

Although it is difficult to meet everyone's needs, a healthy church will offer a variety of ways that people can participate. But take care to keep a balance in the types of events offered. Too much of one event and not enough of another can keep a church from growing. For example, a church with Sunday worship as their only Come Level event and one Sunday school class as their Explore Level event, will not thrive as well as a church that offers two Sunday school classes in addition to the regular worship service, and an outreach program, such as a food pantry. For a small church, this might mean that in addition to the Sunday service and Sunday school classes, the church may want to consider offering a midweek Bible study (which could be a combination Explore/Grow Level event) and an outreach activity, retreat, or another Grow Level event once a quarter. Special holiday services or a church bazaar could serve as additional Come Level events.

If your church doesn't have any events at the Explore Level or the Grow Level, hold a meeting and ask members their preferences. Perhaps give them several choices to consider for both Explore Level and Grow Level events. You may discover that some of your members would like to go on a prayer retreat or form a book group to read and discuss popular books. Don't be afraid to try new and creative ideas: some groups have volunteered at an animal shelter while studying about the Christian's role in caring for creation, learned computer skills together then taught them to women at a local shelter, or watched travel videos and studied travel magazines as a way of learning more about the work of missionaries in certain parts of the world. Remember, a group or class can meet with as few as three members.

# Invite People and Then Invite Them Again

Even if you seem to be repeating yourself at each Sunday service, remind everyone of all upcoming Come Level, Explore Level, and Grow Level events and make sure that they know that anyone is welcome to attend and that no special invitation is needed. Too often small group meetings or Sunday school classes are mentioned only outside of the Sunday service and only to established members. This gives new members and visitors the impression that they need an invitation to attend these events. Announcement time during the Sunday service is a good place to keep people informed, but so is the church's newsletter, flyers on the church's bulletin boards or inserted in the Sunday bulletin, or even notices in the local newspaper.

# How Does a Group of People Become a Church?

For a group of people to become a church, they need to have several things in common: rituals, practices, beliefs, and a common vision. At Seaside Church, the congregation started as individual groups who shared the same beliefs (from the in-home Bible studies), then a particular desire to become a church. Now Pastor Stevens needs to help the individual groups become a community. He can do this by introducing rituals and practices. But he also needs to plan events that encourage the members of the individual groups to interact with each other, so they can better get to know one another.

For the first three months, Seaside offered only a Sunday worship service. Then after meeting with the church's leaders to get input on preferences, Pastor Stevens decided the church needed more Come Level events, as well as some Explore Level events. So he charted a plan for what the church schedule might look like in a year's time:

Sundays:

Informal Sunday morning coffee and continental breakfast, 8:30-9:00 A.M.
Sunday School, 9:00-9:50 A.M.
Sunday Worship,10:00-11:00 A.M. (with nursery options and children's programming available)

Special event for youth (led by the pastor) every second and fourth Sunday evening, 5:30-7:30 P.M. until an official youth group can be formed.

Monday Evenings:

Set aside for necessary church meetings, planning sessions, and leadership training.

Wednesday Evenings:

Vespers, or an evening prayer service on the beach beside Pier 7 (weather permitting), 6:30–7:00 P.M. Coffee at the Pier 7 Café after the service. In case of rain, the service is held at the church.

Thursday Mornings:

A group of members voted to host the "Social Hour" at the local retirement home every third Thursday morning from 10:00-11:00 A.M.

Saturdays:

The first Saturday of every month would be Movie Night with popcorn
and a discussion, sometimes led by a guest speaker, following the movie.
(For example, Pastor Stevens showed *Schindler's List* and invited a guest
speaker who had knowledge of the Holocaust.)
    Every third Saturday evening Seaside hosts a themed potluck dinner.
Nursery and babysitting with special programming are available for
children.

Pastor Stevens's six-month goal was to have all of the Sunday activities in
place, as well as the Thursday social hour at the retirement home and the regular Monday night meetings. Then after these activities were running smoothly,
he planned to begin the Saturday movie nights and potlucks, hopefully by the
end of the year. And once these were in place, he intended to add the
Wednesday night services on the pier.

# Building and Sustaining a Strong Community

Once the church is more established, Pastor Stevens will want to continue to
invite Seaside to strengthen and grow. Pastor Stevens can do this by encouraging
the different residents of Seaside to intermingle and socialize with one another, by
reminding everyone to welcome new members and then help these members con-
nect with groups that best fit their interests, and finally by finding some projects
the church can embrace together as a whole. Let's take a closer look at each one:

1. *Mix it up!* Many churches have small groups that stay separate from
   the church community at large, or groups that attract members of a
   certain age but rarely anyone outside that age group. As a pastor it is
   important for you to look for opportunities to encourage your
   church's members and groups to intermingle. At Seaside, Pastor
   Stevens already has several places where he can start to intermix different ages and different groups. For example, he could invite the
   members who host the Social Hour to plan a party for the youth

group or a children's Sunday school class, or he could have the youth group team up with the Social Hour folks and "adopt a grandparent" at the nursing home. He might suggest that the youth host one of the themed potluck dinners or a movie night, where they could share and discuss one of their favorite movies with the adults. For holidays, the youth could go caroling at the nursing home, or the youth and adults combined could go caroling in the community. Adults in the church might have a special holiday or an interesting career to share with the youth. Pastor Stevens could even suggest that two of the in-home study groups work together on a project, like decorating the sanctuary for the holidays.

2. *Welcome new members.* It is important to list all church groups, along with appropriate contact information and meeting times, in the church's newsletter and on the back of the church's bulletin. Invite each group, committee, and Sunday school class to write up a brief, one-paragraph description of themselves, along with their meeting times and contact information, so that it can be included in a visitor's brochure or new member's packet. Be sure to let visitors and new members know about all of the opportunities your church has to offer and have people available to help them explore these options. Never underestimate the power of a proper introduction.

3. *Initiate churchwide projects.* At least once a year suggest a project on which all of the church's members can work together. Some churches find that making and delivering food baskets at the holidays not only helps them bond as a community, but also gives them a sense of mission. Other churchwide projects can include a clean-up day where the church is thoroughly cleaned, Sunday school rooms are decorated and painted, and any needed repairs are made; or a church yard and bake sale; or a goal to collect a certain number of canned goods, which the church will then deliver to the local food bank. Whatever the project, have the members plan the event well ahead of time and encourage everyone to get involved.

# Icebreakers and Group Activities

*Icebreakers* are structured exercises that encourage people to break the ice and get better acquainted. Icebreakers can be used with any size crowd and are most helpful at Explore Level events to promote fellowship, focus, and to energize the group.

For example, Pastor Stevens surprised the guests at the first potluck with place mats that were also instructions for a game: a scavenger hunt. In addition to hiding some objects around the church (and giving creative clues to where the objects were hidden), he also had people search for information: find a person here tonight whose favorite color is orange, find someone who has owned more than five pets, find a woman who regularly watches golf on television, find out who has taken the most exotic vacation or has traveled the farthest distance.

To begin the first leadership workshop, Pastor Stevens asked leaders to imagine that they, as a group, were going to be dropped off on a deserted island for a six-month stay. Each person could bring with them one person whom they believed possessed the qualities necessary to help organize, motivate, focus, and sustain the group as they tried to survive. Then he asked each person to share whom they had chosen.

*Group Activities* are exercises that encourage communication and interaction on a deeper level. Group Activities can be used at the Explore Level for members who are past the initial phase of meeting and becoming acquainted, and at the Grow Level to help people take the next step in their relationship.

For example, after Seaside's worship committee had met together a couple of times, Pastor Stevens brought in pictures of different sanctuaries and placed them around the room. Each committee member was asked to choose one picture and to spend a period of time, alone, looking at it. Once the group came back together he asked each to share something about their picture, their experience, and their overall feeling of that sanctuary. Did they find it warm and inviting? Stark or cold? Peaceful or unpleasant? Why did they feel this way? In what kind of sanctuary did they typically feel closest to God and why?

# Recruit, Train, and Support Teachers and Leaders

Take the time to support and encourage all of your church's Sunday school teachers, group leaders, and youth and children's ministers. Find ways to help them enhance their leadership skills. Their ability to be faithful and effective leaders is vital to your ministry and your church's overall health and growth.

1. Teach leaders how to use the "Come Level, Explore Level, and Grow Level" model of ministry from this chapter. This can be adapted and used with all age groups and groups of different sizes, and can help leaders vary their leadership style, as well as their group's activities. For example, one Sunday school class can have activities at the various different levels. A suggested pattern for adult Sunday school is to have one Come Level event, two Explore Level events, and one Grow Level event each month.

2. Make sure leaders and teachers know that you are available to help them choose and order educational materials.

3. Offer meetings, workshops, and retreats for leaders and teachers. Invite a guest speaker to discuss a topic that may be of particular concern. Suggest magazines, books, or other leadership training material that can help teachers and leaders avoid burnout or learn more about topics such as how to handle conflict, how to recruit and train helpers and substitute teachers, or ways to energize their ministry.

4. Encourage leaders to attend workshops and seminars offered in your area. Your church may want to start a special fund to offset the cost of workshops so that teachers and group leaders can take advantage of training opportunities that they might not otherwise be able to afford.

5. Look for potential leaders in your congregation. Don't be afraid to ask someone if they would like to be a leader. Sometimes people who won't volunteer to lead a group or teach a class will gladly do so if asked.

6. Make it possible for members to be leaders and teachers without a long-term commitment. Sometimes busy adults feel overwhelmed by the idea of taking on a Sunday school class or group, but would very much like to have the opportunity to teach one or two classes, to be a guest speaker for a special event, or even to be an occasional helper with the youth group. If you get people involved in small ways at first, they are more likely to make a longer commitment in the future.

# Make Time for Youth

If your church doesn't have a youth group or has one that has lost its focus, a good design for youth ministry is the model from this chapter. Just make sure that you offer youth events at all three levels. For example, if your youth group meets weekly, offer two Come Level events, one Explore Level event, and one Grow Level event per month. But don't be afraid to mix these up with youth. Inserting an Explore Level activity inside a Come Level event can be fun for this age group.

Like adults, youth long to be members of a community where they feel valued and accepted. They also want the opportunity to learn and grow in a church that is not afraid to help them find answers to their sometimes hard questions. But too often churches only set aside time for youth on Sunday night with leaders who are untrained volunteers. Did you know that most people decide on their faith and form a relationship with God before the age of eighteen? Be sure to take the faith of children, youth, and young adults seriously. A strong youth ministry requires trained youth leaders and counselors who understand the special developmental, social, and spiritual needs of youth and who are willing to be patient with them.

There are many resources available for training and equipping leaders to work with youth of all ages. Look on the Internet and check out your local Christian bookstore; these are great places to find creative ideas for youth meetings and special activities.

A church that cares about youth will offer several ways for youth to participate in its community. For example, invite youth to serve as liturgists or communion stewards on Sunday morning, publish a special page in the church's newsletter, have youth participate in the choir or form a special youth choir, ask youth to provide special music or perform a short play during Sunday worship, and provide plenty of opportunities for youth to form relationships with adults in the church, and vice versa. To see how well your church incorporates youth, ask yourself:

1. In what ways can youth explore or express their faith in this church?
2. How often are youth invited to participate in the worship service?
3. Can you name at least three ways that youth are valued and accepted in your church, or is your church primarily for adults and young children?
4. Where and to whom can youth bring their questions? Who in your church is available to walk with them on their journey as they struggle to find answers to their difficult questions?

# Keep Children Safe

Many denominations have guidelines for congregations on how to keep children safe. Check with your denomination or church conference for a copy of these guidelines and make sure that anyone who works with children or youth in your congregation has read and understands these guidelines. Briefly, it is recommended that:

1. At least two adults be present at all times with children or youth.
2. Women are counselors for girls, men for boys.
3. Adults leave the door open when talking to youth in a room or office.
4. Parents are clear about what times youth or children's events begin and end.
5. Permission forms are always signed for any events off church property.

6. Touching and hugging are not advised, and hitting a child is never accepted.
7. Parents are notified of any potentially controversial topics to be discussed with youth.
8. If you will be showing a movie or video to youth, parents are informed of the movie's rating, the reason for the rating, and the movie's theme ahead of time.
9. Children or youth are never left alone.
10. Leaders and teachers are aware of any special needs, allergies, or medical conditions of children or youth.

# Pastor's Checklist

1. Everything you need in terms of Icebreakers and Group Activities can be found in *The Encyclopedia of Icebreakers: Structured Activities That Warm-Up, Motivate, Challenge, Acquaint and Energize* by Sue Forbess-Greene (St. Louis: Applied Skills Press, 1980), and *The Encyclopedia of Group Activities: 150 Practical Designs for Successful Facilitating* edited by J. William Pfeiffer (San Diego: University Associates, 1989). Both come in the form of ring binders so that individual pages can be pulled out for group leaders to use.
2. Want to invite a guest speaker? Call community organizations, other churches and pastors, local colleges, senior centers, continuing education programs, lay ministry programs, local missions, or an arts council, to find out who is available in your community and come up with a handy list. Many times, guest speakers will offer their services for free or for a small honorarium.
3. Need something to discuss with teens? Check out what is available in terms of Christian magazines for youth at most online bookstores or at your local Christian bookstore. Many teen magazines are supported by a Web site where you can get leader's guides or questions to use for group discussion.
4. A great novel to discuss with girls ages twelve and up is: *Hope Was Here* by Joan Bauer (New York: Putnam Press, 2000). There is a little bit of everything in this book to talk about: divorce, death, relationships, belief in God, honesty, and integrity.
5. Movie nights can be popular with teens or adults. Movies with Christian themes, such as *The Mission; Brother Sun, Sister Moon; Romero; The Spitfire Grill; The Apostle; Hero* (with Dustin Hoffman); and *The Chosen*, directed by Jeremy Paul Kagan, are good choices.

6. Pastor's book clubs have proved to be popular in some parishes for small groups or even Sunday school classes. Christian or secular books can be used. The following secular books work well for adults (and older teens and college-age students too):

*Saint Maybe* by Anne Tyler (Franklin Library, 1991).

In 1965 the happy Bedloe family is living an ideal "apple pie" existence in Baltimore when a tragic event occurs that forever transforms their lives. Ian Bedloe's response to this tragedy illustrates how participation in a church community shapes our understanding of God, ourselves, and the world in particular ways.

*Etty Hillesum: An Interrupted Life the Diaries, 1941–1943 and Letters from Westerbork* (Henry Holt and Company, 1996).

A young woman in her twenties struggles to rise above all the hate in the midst of the evil and horror of WWII and the Holocaust, and in doing so finds a tremendous inner strength. Her journey from freedom to life in a concentration camp is truly an inspirational faith journey.

*A Map of the World* by Jane Hamilton (Doubleday, 1994).

Alice and Howard Goodwin struggle to make sense of such notions as fate, injustice, evil, forgiveness, and reconciliation. A powerful story of how a single event can transform the lives of everyone involved and change forever the way they understand God and the world.

*North of Hope* by Jon Hassler (Ballantine, 1990).

This is the story of one man's life from childhood to adulthood, and then to ordination into the priesthood and beyond. What this young priest discovers is that God, community, and even love can be found in the most unlikely of places.

*Paradise* by Toni Morrison (A.A. Knopf, 1998).

Following outcasts among the outcast, this difficult novel tells the story of a community of African Americans who have withdrawn from the world (filled as it is with racism and injustice) in order to create an ideal world of their own. But in their new utopia, a town called Ruby, much is revealed about the nature of humanity and the notion of "paradise."

An excellent on-line resource for youth leaders is www.ILeadYouth.com. Network with youth ministers and leaders, get free samples, read related articles, find a list of training events in your area, access master plans for youth ministry and more.

*Children's Ministry Magazine*, an interdenominational magazine for adults who work with children, also hosts a Web site with resources for ministry with children: www.cmmag.com.

---

# CHAPTER NINE

# DO OUTREACH AND MISSION PROJECTS

When Pastor Josie Johnson arrived at Faith Church over a year ago, she faced several challenges. Faith Church, with about eighty-five members in attendance on Sundays, had once been rural, but now it was on the edge of a town that was growing into a small city. Instead of being one of a few churches, as it had been twenty-five years ago, today Faith was one among many churches, most of which were built in the last ten years, and which unlike Faith, had contemporary buildings with modern sanctuaries.

When Josie Johnson received the call to be Faith Church's pastor, its members were mostly farmers, and it had only two mission projects: making and taking holiday food baskets to needy people during the holidays and raising money for the children's wing of the local hospital. Pastor Johnson knew that if Faith Church wanted to survive and thrive, changes would be necessary. The church needed to reach out to the factory workers and business people who populated the growing city. So after taking a year to get to know her congregation, and after preparing them for change, Pastor Johnson felt that Faith was now ready for some new outreach and mission projects. But what projects and how many?

## Keep the Balance

Whatever your church's circumstance, whether similar to Pastor Johnson's or not, try to keep a balance between encouraging your congregation to maintain a strong, faithful bond among its current members on the one hand, and inspiring them to reach out and invite new members on the other. A church that focuses on community building without doing any outreach, or that does outreach without first building a strong community, will either turn inward to the point that it becomes a closed community or it will reach out and extend itself to the point where it loses its particular identity.

# What Does Your Church Have to Offer?

Just as you would not invite friends to a holiday party, then have no one to greet them at the front door and no food to serve them once inside, a church does not want to invite guests to attend if it is not willing to welcome them and help incorporate them into the community. Thus it is important not to reach out to people until you have something to offer. For example, some churches invite young couples with children with the hope that they can gather enough children (and resources from the parents) to have a children's program. But if a church does not have an organized children's program in place, then couples with children who visit are not likely to come back.

Is your church prepared to welcome newcomers? Ask yourself:

1. Does the church have an active hospitality committee?
2. Who acts as hosts to newcomers and helps them find Sunday school classes, the nursery, or a seat in the sanctuary?
3. Is there plenty of space for guests' cars in the parking lot?
4. Is there a map of your church available (either on the wall or in a brochure)?
5. Is there a guest book in which people can sign and give their contact information?
6. Is there a brochure or flyer available with your programs and upcoming events plainly listed with descriptions and contact information?
7. Do you know how your members might greet someone who is dirty, dressed shabbily, is of a different race than the majority of your parishioners, or has a visible handicap?
8. Does your church have something for everyone? Is there a nursery, Sunday school classes, a Bible study, a youth group? Is there assistance available for the elderly or the handicapped?
9. Are restrooms clearly marked?
10. Is the building well maintained? Are classrooms, restrooms, and the sanctuary clean and properly furnished?
11. Do members typically sit together in the back of the church, forcing all guests to sit up front, or in another place that sets them apart from the church's members?
12. Can a guest easily navigate your order of worship?

Some pastors find it helpful to ask a couple of friends to pose as guests, attend the church for a few weeks, then share their experience as a way to see if the church is prepared to welcome newcomers.

# Be Intentional about Outreach

If your church is a well-organized and mostly healthy community that is prepared to welcome guests, the next step is to make sure that the members are intentional about the kind of outreach or mission program they want to support. If your church already has an outreach or mission program, ask members if they can describe the program and explain how it fits into the church's overall vision or mission.

There are two types of Christian outreach and mission: evangelism and charitable giving. Christians are called to a life of *evangelism* and are to share the story of the Gospels, the life of Jesus Christ, and to witness to the presence of God in the world. Christians also are called to love the world, even as God loves it, and are to engage in social work and *charitable giving*. It is important for churches to engage in both charitable giving and evangelism; but make sure that whatever your church does in terms of outreach is a good fit with its resources, the overall vision and mission of your church, and the needs of your particular area or community.

A church without any ministries might start with something simple and something in which the whole church can participate, such as adopting a family for which to care during the holidays. Pastors can also help prepare members for evangelicalism by offering a class or workshop that teaches Christians how to share their faith with others.

If your church already has a few programs, instead of starting something new, expand and improve the programs the church already supports. For an example, let's turn again to Pastor Johnson and Faith Church.

Faith Church raised money for the children's wing of the hospital and made holiday baskets and delivered them to needy families during the holidays. Since the church was made up of mostly farmers, the food basket project suited it well. The baskets contained donations from the members' farms, as well as handmade items. Since two of the church's members were employed by social services, they were able to supply the names, addresses, and requests of families in need. Each year Faith Church assembled the baskets, then delivered them a few days before Thanksgiving and Christmas. This project is an example of *charitable giving*.

The church also raised money for children's ministry by holding an annual rummage and bake sale. The profits from this sale were sent to the local hospital's hospitality room for ill children and their families. This too is an example of *charitable giving*.

Pastor Johnson praised her congregation's efforts, but she also challenged them to consider expanding their ministries to include *evangelism*. She suggested members design an attractive brochure that they could put in each food basket with information about the church, a statement about the church's vision and mission, contact information, as well as a special, handwritten invitation to attend the church. Pastor Johnson also asked members to consider caroling at Christmastime in neighborhoods where the baskets were delivered or in a neighborhood near the church. While caroling, she and the members could hand out flyers, invite people to come to the church, and share something about the upcoming Christmas Eve service.

In terms of sending money to the hospital, Pastor Johnson called and asked if there were any opportunities for church groups to visit with the children or their families. She discovered that the hospital needed volunteers to act as hosts in the children's hospitality room, supply snacks, do crafts, and read to the children. So Pastor Johnson suggested that the women who already met at the church each month to make scrapbooks and note cards might want to consider volunteering at the hospital at least four times a year to teach the children how to decorate angel cards. They could also read stories about angels to the children. Pastor Johnson even offered to use some of the money in her discretionary fund to order some "Faith Church" tee shirts for volunteers to wear to the hospital. This measure would serve as an indirect invitation for the children and their parents to ask about the church. Additionally, Johnson mentioned that this might be a good outreach project for youth, young adults, and other church members as well.

By suggesting ways that Faith Church could expand their outreach and mission projects to include evangelism, Pastor Johnson offered members a chance to minister to people one-on-one, share their faith with others, and establish new relationships. This gave Faith Church an opportunity to become more visible in the community.

# Advertising and Publicity as Outreach

Whether you live in a rural area or in a big city, it is important for a church to be seen and heard. People are more likely to attend if they have heard about your church; seen an ad, flyer, or brochure; or if they have met one of its members. For example, anyone who encounters Faith Church members taking baskets to the needy, or caroling, or sees them at the hospital wearing their church shirts and spending time with the children is more likely to recognize the church's name, ask questions, and attend a Sunday service.

In addition to offering outreach and mission programs, any church that wants to attract new members will want to consider an advertising and publicity campaign. Flyers posted and handed out in your community, ads in the local newspaper or on radio stations (free or paid), articles in the newspaper, or even a mention on television can serve to introduce your church to the community, let people know more about who you are and what you do, and act as an invitation to attend or join. Hosting a church Web page is another way churches can invite people to make a connection with the pastor and members, find out about the church's upcoming events, and see a picture of the church.

Some pastors feel that advertising is a waste of time and money, often saying, "We took out a few ads in the paper, but nothing ever came of it." But a few ads in the paper is *not* an advertising campaign. For advertising to be effective, it must be repeated over an extended period of time; all the ads must have a similar theme, design, and message; and they must reveal something about your church and its vision or mission. Let's turn again to Faith Church.

Pastor Johnson knew that she could not compete with some of the newer and larger churches in the area with their ample advertising budgets, but she knew that she could learn something from taking a closer look at how they advertised and then try to do something similar at Faith Church. She also checked out some advertising and marketing books from the library and searched for additional resources on-line. Here is what she discovered:

1. It is important for a church to know who it is, its vision and mission, *before* it advertises so that it can include this information in its ads.
2. Ads must be attractively designed and appealing. A plain postcard or flyer with just the church's name and contact information is not enough. It is important to be creative, to reveal who you are as a community, and to include a map or directions to the church.
3. An advertising campaign works best when it uses the same logo, catchphrase, or message on all of the ads for at least one campaign. This will give your church a distinct identity, and people who view the ads repeatedly are more likely to remember your chuch.
4. Ads must make a single point and make it powerfully. But ads need not look or sound like ads—sometimes eye-catching pictures or graphics can communicate something about your church better than words or the traditional religion page ad.
5. Ads must be truthful. If your church community is not a contemporary church with plenty of programs for children, do not state or imply this, even if your strongest desire is to attract parents and children.
6. A monthly, personal invitation over a period of three to six months, in the form of a creatively designed postcard or flyer, mailed to people in your church's zip code or to people who have just moved into your community, has proven to be an effective way to advertise.
7. Although most newspapers offer a special advertising section for churches at a discounted rate, look for additional ways to advertise,

perhaps by choosing another section of the paper. For example, if you have an upcoming concert, you might want to consider placing an ad in the arts and entertainment section of the newspaper.

8. Take advantage of free advertising. Press releases can prompt the media to feature your church in the news for free. Send press releases to newspapers, radio, and television stations if:

- You have an upcoming special event
- There is someone in your church who is doing something unique or of interest to the community
- Your church is celebrating a milestone
- You are holding a special fund-raiser for an organization in the community
- There has been a tragic event that is of interest to the community at large
- Someone in your church has a special connection to a story in the local, state, or national news
- If your church is doing a project that is of interest to the community, such as building a Habitat for Humanity House or offering a grief support group.

9. It is important to send out press releases one month prior to the date of the upcoming event.
10. Some local radio, television stations, and newspapers carry public service announcements for free. Consider having your church sponsor a public service announcement.

# Plan an Advertising Campaign

Remember, an advertising campaign is a group effort. Three or more people will be needed to organize and oversee the campaign. At Faith Church, Pastor Johnson called upon seven of the more creative members, and with help from a member's grandson who was studying marketing in college, they formed a committee and came up with a six-month plan:

**Faith Church: You're Welcome/Smiley Face Advertising Campaign.**

Goals: (1) Design, post, and distribute flyers from August through January promoting the church in the community. (2) Advertise the Fall Rummage and Bake Sale, the Annual Turkey Fund-raising Dinner, and the Christmas Eve service. (3) Place at least three consecutive ads (one each week around the Thanksgiving/Christmas Holiday time) in the local newspaper. (4) Choose 100 addresses in an area near the church and mail one postcard or flyer each month for three months. (5) Send out press releases to local media about happenings in the church. (6) Sponsor a "Don't Drink and Drive" community service announcement for the holidays. (7) Design and post a church Web page. (8) Come up with at least one unconventional way to invite people to come to church.

Budget: $500

Sample Ad for Newspaper:

You're Welcome.

Faith Church
1500 Davis Road
Corner of Davis & Sr26

www.FaithChurchWired.org
(555) 555-1500

The Faith Church Advertising Committee also used a version of the "You're Welcome/Smiley Face" design on all of its postcards, posters, flyers, newsletters, brochures, stationery, as well as on its Web page. For their one unconventional way to invite people to church, the committee had the "You're Welcome/Smiley Face" logo without the church's name printed on large, plastic buttons. They asked members to wear the buttons on their jackets from August through January. Whenever anyone asked about the button, the church member would share something about their faith and the church, and invite the person to attend. The committee also planned to meet and evaluate the advertising campaign once it ended.

# Send Out Media Releases

Keep handy a list of contact information for local television and radio stations (especially Christian radio stations), as well as both print and online media, so that anytime your church has an event or announcement, it can be sent quickly. It is important to keep the list updated, with the correct names, street addresses, e-mails addresses, and phone and fax numbers. Here's a sample press release that Faith Church sent to local newspapers, radio, and television stations to advertise their rummage and bake sale:

Press Release

Date: Sept. 15

Contact: Ed Duncan, Faith Church Publicity Committee (555) 555-1234

Faith Church Hosts Fund-raiser for Children's Hospitality Room at Westside Hospital

Faith Church will host its annual rummage and bake sale from 8:00 A.M. to 3:00 P.M. on Saturday, October 15, at the church, 1500 Davis Road (corner of Davis and SR 26). Come rain or shine. The profits from this sale will go to the Children's Hospitality Room at Westside Hospital, a room staffed by volunteers to offer comfort and support to ill children and their families. Faith Church supports the Children's Hospitality Room by holding this fund-raiser and by volunteering to staff the room and do craft projects with the children. For more information, please contact Pastor Josie Johnson at (555) 555-1500 or visit www.FaithChurchWired.org.

# Public Service Announcements

Call first to see if the media in your area accept public service announcements (PSAs). If they do, many national organizations and denominations have PSAs available for free. Often, space is provided where local churches that sponsor the PSA can add a line or a statement with their name and contact information at the end. Local organizations, such as an animal shelter with an adopt-a-homeless-pet campaign or a fire station holding a fire safety campaign, might also be willing to partner with a local church on a PSA. Churches can record or design their own PSAs, but note, these must *not* be advertisements for your church, but rather announcements that are beneficial to the public. PSAs are typically carried by many electronic media (television, radio, and online) free of charge. You supply the appropriate person with the announcement and then update it when needed.

Since Faith Church had voted to sponsor a "Don't Drink and Drive" PSA, they contacted the local chapter of Mothers Against Drunk Driving (MADD) and partnered with them to send out announcements to the local media. MADD had a recorded announcement, as well as some predesigned print ads, for Faith Church to use. They sent the ads to Faith Church, who then added a ten-second "statement of sponsorship" at the end of each: "This public service announcement was brought to you by Faith Church. For more information, please visit our Web site: www.FaithChurchWired.org." They added similar information to the bottom of the print ads. Then one month prior to the Thanksgiving, Christmas, and New Year's holidays, they took the audio recordings to the local radio stations and sent the print ads to local newspapers. (Note: Television stations require an even longer lead time before running PSAs, usually two to three months.) To complement the radio announcements and print ads, Faith Church also posted a message encouraging people to not drink and drive and a link to MADD on their Web site.

# Encourage Guests to Become Members

If a church wants to turn guests into members, it will need to take seriously the practice of greeting, welcoming, and assimilating them into the congregation. Encouraging guests to become members is the responsibility of the whole church and not simply the pastor's. But you can help your church become one that turns guests into members by affirming the practice of hospitality in your sermons, messages, and classes, and by holding meetings or workshops to teach members how to reach out to newcomers. For example, your members can:

- Greet guests
- Answer any questions that guests may have
- Help newcomers find their way around the church
- Introduce guests to other members of the church
- Follow up with guests after their visits
- Make sure newcomers are invited back, as well as to any upcoming events

Here are some dos and don'ts for encouraging guests to become members:

- Don't make guests wear name tags, sit in a special place, raise their hands, stand up during the service, or try to figure out who's who at your church. Instead, have your greeters and church leaders wear name tags with their name and title every week. Have hosts greet guests with statements such as, "My name is _____. If there is anything I can get you, or any question I can answer for you, please don't hesitate to ask me." Have the hosts or ushers' help the guests find their seats. Ushers will also want to follow up with guests after the service by giving them one of the church's brochures and perhaps offering them a cup of coffee or inviting them to lunch.

- Don't comment on the way people are dressed, ask personal questions, try to make a joke, or be too pushy. Always use common sense and keep initial conversations upbeat, friendly, and focused on making the guest feel valued and welcomed.
- Do plan a fun group activity for a leadership retreat or church meeting to role-play welcoming guests. Encourage leaders and church members to practice on their own too. Not everyone is comfortable with talking to strangers, but members who practice welcoming guests will be more comfortable and, consequently, the guests will feel more welcome too.
- Do make sure that guests are not only warmly received at your Sunday service, but also Sunday school classes, small group meetings, and other events. Suggest that members of classes and groups make a point to welcome guests, wear name tags when a guest is present, and to smile, make eye contact, and include the guest in the discussion or activity.
- Do greet youth and children, not just their parents.
- Do acknowledge guests from the pulpit, but do it in a general way: "We are blessed to have some guests with us today. Let me welcome you and also remind you that you are invited to attend any of the classes, groups, or upcoming events at our church."
- Do make sure guests know that you are glad they came. Have greeters, leaders, and church members say things such as, "Thank you for visiting our community," or "I am glad you came. If I can help you in any way, please just let me know."
- Do follow-ups with guests within one to two days. A phone call or handwritten note needs to tell them that you are pleased they chose to visit, that you hope they will come again, and that you will be happy to provide them with more information. All they need to do is ask. Remember, it is not the sole responsibility of the pastor to greet guests, welcome them, or to try and assimilate them into the community. This is a churchwide responsibility.
- Do always follow up with new members three months after they join to make sure they are making connections and being properly assimilated into the community.

# Pastor's Checklist

1. Check and see that your church's newsletter is clear, concise, and informative. The newsletter should be:

   - Positive in tone with any negative information kept to a minimum
   - Effortless to read—use the same font throughout and space appropriately
   - Consistent—use the same format and similar graphics each month
   - Include your mission statement, contact information, and upcoming events (up to two months in advance)

2. Check out free items for churches available on the Internet: Web page templates, Web space, clip art, graphics, Christian quotes, comics, inspirational stories for newsletters, and ideas or opportunities for mission and outreach programs. Do a search for keywords such as Christian clip art, quotes, missions, or free Web space for churches.

3. Internet search engines offer free message boards, e-mail lists or groups, and chat rooms. Churches can use these to post online newsletters, invite prayer requests or host a prayer chain, set up an online community for youth, or keep in touch with seniors, or members who are ill, homebound, or out-of-town.

4. Be seen and heard! Pastors who participate in mission and outreach programs, online message boards, chats, prayer chains, and who write a pastor's page for their newsletter are more likely to have an influential voice in their church's "community conversation."

*Speaking Faith: The Essential Handbook for Religious Communicators*, 7th edition. Religious Communicators Council (475 Riverside Drive, Rm. 1355, New York, NY 10115, www.religioncommunicators.org).

This is an easy-to-read book with step-by-step instructions on how to choose and undertake an advertising campaign, send out press releases, do interviews with the press, set up a Web page, design a professional-looking newsletter and much more. The book comes with a compact disc with worksheets and training materials so you can use the information on your computer. This book can easily help you set up a comprehensive advertising and publicity campaign for your church (no matter what its size).

Yvon Prehn. *Ministry Marketing Made Easy: A Practical Guide to Marketing Your Church Message*. Abingdon Press, 2004.

This book provides specific tips for how to set up a clear, positive, and consistent marketing strategy for your church.

Robin Williams. *The Non-Designer's Design Book*. Peachpit Press, 2004.

Robin Williams and John Tollett. *The Non-Designer's Web Book*. Peachpit Press, 2000.

Is your church's newsletter or Web page attractive and simple to navigate? These user-friendly books will teach you everything you need to know to design a professional-looking newsletter or design and post an attractive Web page.

CONCLUSION

# MINISTRY IS A JOURNEY

Remember, ministry is a journey, not a destination. Too many pastors make the mistake of judging their ministry in terms of whether they have arrived at a particular place: whether their church is healthy, productive, faithful, and growing. But if you strive for perfection, you will be disappointed. In the end, more important than where you *arrive* in your ministry are the *steps* you take along the way.

Each church you serve will be at a different place on its journey: some churches will be thriving, some struggling, and some dying. No matter what, the pastor's job is to foster theological and spiritual growth. The fruits of this labor, however small, will always be visible in at least some of the members at each church you serve.

Keep in mind too that your congregation's trust, while essential to your ministry, can only be earned over time. Only when a congregation becomes convinced that you, as their pastor, *truly* care about them, will they trust you. But once trust is established, a congregation *will* be accepting and forgiving. In fact, there are many examples of pastors who are disorganized administrators or boring preachers, but their churches still love them and are willing to follow their lead. Members still grow under these ministers' care because they are assured of their pastor's devotion.

Finally, at each stop in your journey, take the time to celebrate the victories, however small, and be grateful for each person and each church you serve along the way, for they stand at the heart of your vocation, and your relationship with them is the context in which you meet God.